WELLNESS
WARRIOR STYLE

WELLNESS
WARRIOR
STYLE

A Simple, Peer-Supported Guide
to Help First Responders
and Veterans Heal

KIM COLEGROVE

mango
PUBLISHING

CORAL GABLES

Cover & Layout Design: Megan Werner
Cover Illustration: Levin / stock.adobe.com

For permission requests, please contact the publisher at:
Mango Publishing Group
2850 S Douglas Road, 2nd Floor
Coral Gables, FL 33134 USA
info@mango.bz

For special orders, quantity sales, course adoptions and corporate sales, please email the publisher at sales@mango.bz. For trade and wholesale sales, please contact Ingram Publisher Services at customer.service@ingramcontent.com or +1.800.509.4887.

Wellness Warrior Style: A Simple, Peer-Supported Guide to Help First Responders and Veterans Heal

Library of Congress Cataloging-in-Publication number: 2023943714
ISBN: (pb) 978-1-68481-326-1 (hc) 978-1-68481-327-8
(e) 978-1-68481-328-5
BISAC category code: SEL043000, SELF-HELP /
Post-Traumatic Stress Disorder (PTSD)

This book is dedicated to

David M. Colegrove

CONTENTS

FOREWORD

In every community, small rural towns to big cities, some of our neighbors are first responders. Firefighters, law enforcement, dispatchers, paramedics, ER doctors, nurses, and many more folks choose to dedicate their lives to helping others. Most of us have members of the military in our families, including veterans. All of these people serve our country and our communities and have sacrificed much to help all of us. While I am sure they would agree there is no more important kind of work, it could also be said that this is one of the most stressful and arduous kinds of work. Coming from a military family, I have seen the effect this kind of trauma has on warriors. I became aware of Kim Colegrove's work with Pause First Academy and have read her books which have saved lives of warriors who, as stoics do, try to tough it out on their own until they feel they have nowhere to turn. Thank goodness they found Kim's book, *The Mindfulness for Warriors Handbook*. My great hope is that even more find *Wellness Warrior Style,* which offers profoundly helpful practices and empowering stories of warriors who faced their trauma and reclaimed their mental wellness and their lives in the process. I could not be more proud of Kim and how she gives back to those who give so much.

My dad, Walter, was a Marine who enlisted right before his eighteenth birthday. Growing up on a farm in Kentucky didn't prepare him for what he saw on the battlefields of World War II. He went to war as a boy and came back a man, albeit one with a lot of shock and pain because of what he saw and experienced in Japan. This was, of course, before the concept of Post-Traumatic Stress even existed. PTSD was recognized by advocates, physicians, military veterans, and activists after lengthy activism on behalf of Vietnam veterans, many of whom came home from war in deep distress. Physical wounds are very grave, and layering on psychological wounds makes a return to regular life nearly impossible. One of my uncles, a naval officer, used to say "You can leave the war, but the war might not leave you." Veterans are the first responders of our nation; they defend our country and rush into battle to defend all of us.

Other first responders also rush in wherever help is needed and go where others fear to tread. Firefighters, police officers, EMTs, emergency room staff, and many more folks deal with high-stress situations where others lives depend on them. Those who retired from these roles don't magically release their trauma when they leave the job. In fact, it is often compounded, because you no longer have your friends and coworkers with whom you can talk and let off steam or share a sense of camaraderie.

No one knows this more than author Kim Colegrove. Her beloved husband, Dave, was a law enforcement officer who retired after dedicating decades to his career. He retired and, after three months to the shock of his family and friends, took his own life. He quit the job, but the job didn't quit him. All that stress and pain, built up over years, had no outlet. He made a choice, one we never want a loved one to make.

This book is intended to help the helpers.

This book is intended to provide outlets.

This book provides tools to deal and heal the trauma.

If you know a veteran or a retiree or have a loved one serving our country who can use some stress relief, gift them this book. I have gifted copies to my local police, firefighters, and also a dispatcher who would start tearing up when she talked about some of the calls she gets. Dispatchers are first responders, too.

Be well,

Becca Anderson, author of *Badass Affirmations*

INTRODUCTION

For those of you who are not familiar with my work, I'll start by introducing myself. I'm the author of *Mindfulness for Warriors* and *The Mindfulness for Warriors Handbook*, and I'm the owner of Pause First Academy—an organization created to provide holistic wellness and resilience training for society's warriors, protectors, guardians, and healers.

Prior to this work, I was a meditation and mindfulness instructor. I taught in corporate settings, worked with private clients, and offered community classes.

I never intended to become a champion for culture change across warrior professions, but after I lost my husband to suicide, less than three months after he retired from a thirty-year law enforcement career, that's exactly what happened.

First, I adapted my meditation and mindfulness training to appeal to first responders and veterans. Then, I expanded my curriculum to include resilience training. Eventually, I invited other instructors to join me and together we created Pause First Academy, where we provide online and in-person training that is specifically tailored to the warrior culture.

Pause First Academy is upgrading and modernizing the way warriors approach well-being. We focus on holistic wellness, resilience, and work-life balance. Our online service is subscription-based and is available to organizations and individuals. Our instructors are culturally competent and most have backgrounds as first responders or veterans.

In the *Mindfulness for Warriors* books, I told the full story and went into detail about my husband David's struggles prior to taking his own life. I also shared my intimate account of the aftermath and why I decided to step into this arena.

In this book, I'm going to focus more on *your* journey. My goal is for this book to provide a safe space for you to privately consider the inner mental and emotional turmoil you've experienced, and to contemplate ways to bolster your health and well-being.

Just as I did before, I've enlisted a group of warriors to help me with this goal. In total, I interviewed fourteen people for this book. Each one has a powerful story and an important perspective.

One last thing I'll share with you before we jump into the book is my work with an organization called The Battle Within. The Battle Within is based in Kansas City, Missouri, and offers a free five-day group therapy program to help warriors understand the traumas they have endured, learn integrative healing tools, and develop a community of support.

Since 2018, I have provided meditation and mindfulness instruction for The Battle Within cohorts. It is absolutely some of my favorite work, and I believe wholeheartedly in the curriculum, mission, and efficacy of this organization. In this book, you'll meet a couple of alumni of the program, as well as the executive director and the clinical director. There's more information about TBW in the resource directory at the back of this book.

And now, I'm happy to present to you:, *Wellness Warrior Style*. May you find hope, inspiration, and motivation within these pages. You deserve to live and retire healthfully. No matter where you are on your life's journey, please know that it's never too late to step onto a healing path.

On the next page you'll find a song that was written by nine veterans during a healing excursion. My friend Mhanu was one of the contributors, and graciously shared the lyrics with me after he left the retreat. I was so moved by this piece that I asked Mhanu if he and the others would consider giving me permission to share the song as a poem in my book. The chorus of the song comes in after every eight lines, but I have placed the chorus at the end of the poem for the purposes of this book.

WEATHER'S GONNA BREAK

I'm better but still hurting
I'm learning to see again
Optimistically uncertain
And I'm facing all my sins

I'm finding myself
In the whisper of the ashes
Rising like a phoenix
Sending them demons crashing

The last war I came home from
Wasn't the last I had to fight
Drowning my sorrows in a bottle
Cranking that throttle and wrecking my life

The shadows were chasing me
For as long as I remember
But I'm feeling the seasons changing
Like the leaves of September

I can breathe again
There's a parting in the grey
I'm vibing and I'm healing
Sunshine's finally on my face
There's gonna be some better days

I'm pulling back my bow and letting go
of the guilt and the shame—
Got a quiver full of lightning
I'm torn but I'm fighting for change

I've been a thunderhead of chaos
And I've had all that I can take
Now I know the weather's gonna break
I can see the weather's gonna break

Written by: Thomas Harris, Jeremiah Lord, Mhanu Boulengier, Matt Merriman, Dave Johnson, Matt Schiefer, Paul Slough, Tyler Kuhn, and Jay Clementi.

Thank you to each of you for allowing me to share these lyrics as a poem. And thank you to my friend Mhanu Boulengier, for trusting me, for staying in touch, for sharing your journey with me, and for giving of yourself to help others.

PART I
CROSSROADS

CHAPTER 1

GETTING ORIENTED

—

WELLNESS

In this book, I'm primarily focusing on mental and emotional wellness, not so much on physical health. Why? While movement and nutrition are important facets of wellness, fitness and diet information is ubiquitous and readily available. Most warriors understand the importance of staying physically fit, and know that diet and nutrition are crucial components of physical health.

I have chosen to zero in on the elements of well-being that have traditionally been overlooked across all warrior professions: mental and emotional health. I want to help you understand that you cannot separate mental and emotional health from physical health. It's all part of your *health*. It's interconnected. You can't just exercise and keep your body fit while neglecting your mind and emotions. That will inevitably create imbalance. Until recently, imbalance has been the status quo. If you're feeling this, I want to help you bring yourself and your life into better balance.

WARRIOR STYLE

Please don't get hung up on the words *warrior*, *first responder*, or *veteran*. In this book, you are all warriors. In fact, below, I have provided a list of folks I'm including when I use the term *warrior*.

Whether you're active military, a veteran, a dispatcher, a correctional officer, a victim advocate, or a firefighter, in this context, you are a warrior. These are all very different professions, I know. But trauma did not get that memo. There are similarities across these professions that beg for wellness to be delivered *warrior style*, and that's what this book delivers.

You are not like average people. You are human beings who have done extremely difficult and traumatizing work, and trauma has infiltrated your world, no matter what your title is.

To help make this point, here is *my* definition of a warrior: A warrior is anyone who stands ready to serve, protect, and defend a person, place, thing, or cause, and will fight and sacrifice for the betterment of others and for the greater good.

Here is a non-exhaustive list of professions I consider to be warriors, in no particular order:

1. Military personnel (Army, Navy, Air Force, Marines, Space Force)
2. Law enforcement officers
3. Dispatchers
4. Firefighters
5. Paramedics and EMTs
6. Correctional officers
7. Parole officers
8. Probation officers
9. Victim advocates
10. Social workers
11. Healthcare professionals (doctors, nurses, surgeons)
12. Hospital staff (technicians,

pharmacists, administrative staff)

13. Mental health counselors and therapists

14. Coast Guard personnel

15. Search and rescue teams

16. Security personnel (private and public)

17. Hazardous materials (HazMat) response teams

18. Crisis intervention teams

19. Peer support specialists and teams

20. Disaster response teams

21. Lifeguards

22. Emergency management personnel

23. Crisis counselors

24. Chaplains and other spiritual care providers

25. Disaster relief volunteers

26. Rehabilitation specialists

27. Public defenders and prosecutors

28. Hospice workers/end-of-life care specialists

RESILIENCE

At the heart of this discussion about wellness is resilience. What do you think of when you hear the word *resilience*? I've posited this question in my classes many times over the years. I usually get answers like, being able to take a punch, or, getting back up when you've been knocked down. This is part of resilience, for sure. But, maybe, there's a little more to resilience than just being able to survive a beatdown.

One of my favorite definitions of resilience is the one my friend and colleague Brenda Dietzman uses in her presentations:

Resilience is the capacity to prepare for, cope with, and grow through adversity.

This book aims to help you develop a new understanding of resilience. It's full of ideas for rebuilding your inner reserves and developing the ability to prepare for, cope with, and grow through adversity. You'll start with healing trauma and build from there.

I hope you'll let me and the fourteen warriors I interviewed help you find ways to reach out for help, heal any existing trauma, learn new integrative skills and practices, and navigate resilience in a whole new way.

CHAPTER 2

ASSESSING WHERE YOU ARE

—

SELF-REFLECTION: THE FIRST STEP TO HEALING

Step one on the journey to well-being is self-reflection. This will require honesty and a bit of vulnerability. Self-reflection is a powerful tool in the process of determining where you are in life compared to where you want to be.

Here are some questions you might ask yourself:

- *Am I happy?*

- *How's my mental health?*

- *How's my emotional health?*

- *Have I been ignoring or suppressing my emotions?*

- *Am I at peace and satisfied with my work, relationships, and overall quality of life?*

- *How have my experiences on the job affected me?*

- *Am I carrying the weight of unresolved trauma or grief?*

Your answers may be painful, but they can also be liberating, and they can help you make a decision about seeking support. Contemplating these questions can help pave the way to your personal crossroads, the point at which you decide to step away from survival mode and take the first few steps toward truly living this one precious life.

Self-reflection involves a compassionate and honest look at yourself. Take a moment to think about how you've been feeling lately. Have you noticed any problems with your mood, behavior, or sleep patterns? Are you struggling with burnout or compassion fatigue? Have friends, family members, or colleagues expressed concern about you? These observations are valuable indicators of your current state of well-being.

You'll also want to consider factors outside of your profession that may have contributed to how you're feeling. While the demands of your job are or were (if you're retired) undoubtedly significant, it's essential to acknowledge that external factors, such as adverse childhood experiences, personal relationships, financial pressures, and life events, can also play a role in your overall state of wellness. Acknowledging these influences will help you create a more comprehensive assessment.

As you make your assessment, it's crucial to factor in mental and emotional health, physical health, the health of your relationships, and your overall quality of life. Common issues among warriors are anxiety, depression, substance abuse, risky behavior, relationship problems, and insomnia. These challenges can infiltrate every area of your life, and, left unchecked, can wreak havoc on your day-to-day quality of life.

THE SILENT STRUGGLES
OF WARRIORS

For first responders, the silent struggles often lurk just beneath the surface, masked by the stoicism and endurance required by the job. They carry a massive weight of responsibility, day in and day out, as they regularly witness dysfunction, violence, and the trauma and suffering of others. The demands of the career necessitate resilience, but the emotional toll of the work almost always wears down that resilience, leaving first responders stressed, traumatized, and hurting on the inside.

Military veterans have their own silent battles. Many return from service having witnessed unbearable atrocities and unspeakable horrors, and some carry the crushing weight of losing friends, sometimes in combat, and way too often to suicide.

These experiences leave indelible scars on the psyche, and both groups—in fact, all warriors—tend to lean on unhealthy coping mechanisms because they don't know how to process and heal the crushing pain they carry.

All warriors have a long history of suffering in silence. Take a moment to assess the struggles you've endured alone and in silence.

THE DARK SHADOW OF STIGMA

Silent suffering thrives in the shadow of stigma—a stigma that often suggests that seeking help is synonymous with weakness. The shadow that hangs over individuals who need help but are afraid to ask for it perpetuates the silence because they fear the judgment of peers and superiors. They worry about potential consequences if they speak up. In both first responder and military cultures, there's a perception that acknowledging mental health challenges shows weakness and destroys careers.

When you think about reaching out or asking for help, do you feel fear and anxiety? Do you worry about retribution, demotion, dismissal, or ridicule? Does the stigma attached to seeking help for mental and emotional suffering prevent you from doing so?

If so, I'm here to call bullshit on that nonsense, and encourage you to take what might be the most courageous step you've ever taken. Seek help and accept support.

CHOOSING THE PATH OF HEALING

Imagine you are standing at a crossroads, a fork in the road. Your choices are to continue down your current path, or step onto the path of healing.

The easier choice is probably to stay on the path you know. It's familiar. There are no surprises. You know what to expect. You've learned to navigate this path, you're don't really have the energy to embark on an unknown path, and you're not even convinced you really *need* the healing path.

As you stand there, finalizing your decision and leaning toward continuing on your current path, you notice that the road ahead looks a little rough. You acknowledge that it's been getting bumpy for a while and now you're wondering just how bad it might get around the bend. You've heard stories about others who insisted on continuing down their own well-worn path and it didn't end well.

This choice is yours to make. It's a choice: to prioritize self-care, confront mental and emotional health concerns, and improve your chances of living and retiring healthfully; or to keep doing what you've been doing and hope for the best.

ENHANCING YOUR QUALITY OF LIFE

Selecting the path of healing signifies a commitment to enhancing the quality of your own life. It's an affirmation that says you believe you deserve happiness, peace, and contentment. Will it be challenging? Maybe. Will you have to step out of your comfort zone? Probably. Will it be worth it? Definitely.

THRIVING IN LIFE AND RETIREMENT

Your life shouldn't be about just surviving. You deserve to thrive. You have given of yourself in order to serve, protect, defend, guard, or save others. It has been draining, and it's time for you to reclaim the vitality you once had. You deserve to live, work, and retire healthfully. Every choice you make on this path is a vote for who you want to be in the future.

In the following chapters, you will learn to navigate the complex terrain of mental health, wellness, resilience, and healing, primarily by reading the stories of some of your peers who chose the path of healing. These are first responders, veterans, and others who understand the difficult way of the warrior. Through their stories, we'll explore the practical strategies, tools, and resources that guided them toward a brighter future.

My hope is that these stories will encourage you to make the choice to honor yourself, defy stigma, and embrace healing. No matter where you are in your career—just starting out, midway, facing retirement, or already retired—I hope you apply the knowledge you gain from this book and create a happier, healthier, more peaceful life.

But to embark on this journey fully, you will need to take off your armor, lay down your shield, and be open to vulnerability. As you will learn from your peers across these pages, vulnerability is not weakness. It requires great strength and courage, and it will be your greatest ally as you walk the path toward healing.

Before you move on to the next chapter, here's another look at the questions to ask yourself:

- Am I happy?

- How's my mental health?

- How's my emotional health?

- Have I been ignoring or suppressing my emotions?

- Am I at peace and satisfied with my work, relationships, and overall quality of life?

- How have my experiences on the job affected me?

- Am I carrying the weight of unresolved trauma or grief?

CHAPTER 3

DECIDING WHERE YOU WANT TO GO

In the previous chapter, we dove into the process of assessing where you are. We addressed some of the typical roadblocks you may have encountered on your path, and discussed some of the benefits you'll have access to if you choose the path of healing.

Now that you've sort of wrapped your mind around where you are in terms of your mental and emotional well-being, level of happiness, and quality of life, I invite you to consider what you'd like your life to look and feel like in the future.

Some of you might be feeling pretty okay as you read this book. Maybe you get a little stressed, you have some hard days, but you're not miserable by any stretch. So far, you've managed to keep your mental and emotional well-being fairly balanced, you have decent self-care practices in place, your relationships are healthy, and you enjoy a good amount of job satisfaction. But the work is starting to take a toll, and you want to learn ways to maintain the quality of life you've established. Good for you for considering the healing path *before* you find yourself in crisis mode. For you, this new path will be a source of prevention and maintenance.

For others, reading this book and considering change is more like a crisis response. You find yourself in some level of personal and/or professional dissatisfaction, you're burned-out, stressed, anxious, or depressed. Maybe the job satisfaction you once experienced is fading or gone. Maybe your personal life is suffering. You aren't well, you aren't happy, and you simply need some relief.

Making the choice to change can be challenging. Most humans are resistant to change. For some reason, we'd rather suffer in our comfort zone than find the courage to step outside that zone of "comfort" and do something different. The comfort zone is often not comfortable at all, it's just familiar. It's what we know, it's our well-worn path, and if we're honest, the unknown feels uncontrollable and scary, so we avoid it.

FACING CHALLENGES

Facing challenges head-on is never easy, especially when those challenges involve the personal aspects of your life. Sure, you've met the demands and challenges of your profession like a warrior. But when it comes to your own self-care, your mental and emotional health, and maybe even your physical health, you haven't invested the time and effort. Why? Because you *are* the help, and in my experience, the helpers tend to neglect themselves.

The decision to confront these personal challenges is an act of courage and self-compassion. It's a declaration that your own well-being is worth the effort, and that you are committed to living a life that is not defined by pain, stress, anxiety, and trauma.

HOLISTIC WELLNESS

Holistic wellness involves addressing your mental, emotional, and physical well-being as interconnected aspects of your overall health. Other considerations in a holistic approach to wellness are your lifestyle, relationships, hobbies, spirituality, and whatever other categories are important to you.

A holistic approach to wellness encompasses practices such as exercise, nutrition, mindfulness, and self-care. When you decide where you want to go on your wellness journey, consider embracing a holistic approach that nourishes not only your mind, but also your body, soul, and everything that makes up the totality of your specific life experience. We're all different. You need to determine what matters to *you*.

Why is a holistic approach necessary? Because, in order to experience balance, contentment, and a better quality of life, you have to bring all of aspects of you onto the path of healing. For example, you can't separate mental health from your overall health. Mental health *is* health. You can be the fittest, strongest, most physically healthy person on the planet, but if your mental and emotional health are left unattended, you will never truly be healthy. You will be out of balance, and that is not sustainable if you also want to be happy and feel good.

THE IMPORTANCE OF SEEKING HELP

We take this journey by ourselves, but never alone. You have to make the decision to step onto a new path, and you have to walk the path on your own two feet, but there will be helpers, guides, mentors, and friends to keep you company along the way.

A journey to wellness often involves seeking help. The form of help you seek is up to you. Talk therapy can be very helpful. Trusted friends and mentors are often pivotal in the process of healing. Treatment facilities and programs help a lot of people heal, recover, and start fresh. Or you can start with your EAP (Employee Assistance Program) if there is one, or reach out to a peer support group.

> *As you start to walk on the way,*
> *the way appears*
> **—Rumi, thirteenth-century poet**

There are a lot of interpretations of this quote, but I take it to mean that you don't have to have everything figured out in order to embark on a journey. All you have to do is decide where you want to go, get pointed in that direction, and take a step.

Think of it like entering a location into the navigation app on your phone. You just type in the name of the place you want to go, then follow the directions provided. Your healing path will be a lot like that. You can't possibly know where the journey between here and there will take you. You can't anticipate every stop and turn, and that's okay because it's not your job to figure that out beforehand. Your job will be to stay on the route and keep moving.

If you need to pause and rest a bit here and there along the way, that's fine. But if you feel yourself turning around and going backward, back to where you came from, back to the people, places, choices, and behaviors that took you down the wrong path to begin with, do whatever you have to do to correct your course and get back on the path and headed in the right direction.

In the chapters ahead, we will explore practical strategies, stories of hope, and inspiring insights to help support your journey to a happier, healthier life. Before moving on to the next page, take a moment, and a few deep breaths. Reflect on where you are and how you've been feeling. Then, allow yourself to imagine how you'd like to feel and where you'd like your life's path to take you. Make some mental notes. See it; picture a future in which you feel balanced, peaceful, and free from the contraction of your current state of discontent.

If you're in such a bad place that you can't see a better future, that's okay too. Many others have been where you are, as you're about to read. You are not alone. Just keep reading and remain open to the idea of accepting the help that's available.

CHAPTER 4

THE JOURNEY BEGINS

The start of any journey can be filled with uncertainty. If you're feeling unsure or hesitant about this, I would say that's normal, especially in the warrior culture. You are accustomed to saving, rescuing, guarding, or defending people, and you're often the solution to other people's problems. You're used to providing help. What you're *not* used to is *needing* help. You aren't comfortable *being* vulnerable, you're comfortable *protecting* the vulnerable.

THE COURAGE TO START

Believe it or not, the courage you need to start the healing process begins with vulnerability. According to researcher and author Brené Brown, "Vulnerability is not winning or losing; it's having the courage to show up and be seen when we have no control over the outcome. Vulnerability is not weakness; it's our greatest measure of courage." By the way, if you aren't familiar with Brené Brown's work, I highly

31

suggest you check out her books. A couple of my favorites are *Daring Greatly* and *The Power of Vulnerability*.

Believe me, I know it is exceptionally difficult for warriors to allow themselves to be vulnerable. You've spent your life developing that hard, impenetrable outer shell of protection and you've learned to never let your guard down. You're vigilant. You're disciplined, brave, and competent. You're a lot of things, but soft is not one of those things.

In your world, vulnerable means soft, maybe even weak. But in reality, vulnerable means human. And you, my friend, are human. Heroes are human. Warriors are human. Each and every warrior is born with the same feelings, emotions, and frailties as the rest of us. However, you have had to deny some of that humanness in favor of surviving.

Some of you have witnessed and endured more stress, trauma, tragedy, violence, death, and destruction in one year, or maybe even one shift, than the rest of us will encounter in a lifetime. So, developing the ability to turn off your humanness and shut down your emotions might have felt like a necessity. However, now, I'd like you to consider the damage that may have done to your well-being.

Growth and healing are not always easy. Your willingness to start this journey is what really makes you brave. That's not just fluffy rhetoric. Anyone can stay stuck, isolate, drink themselves into an early grave, destroy relationships, and become angry, combative shells of who they once were. That's the easy path. That path requires zero self-reflection and no accountability. But it also robs people of what could have been a meaningful, rewarding life.

It takes immense courage to open up, acknowledge your struggles, and seek support.

THE VALUE OF PATIENCE

Healing requires vulnerability, and it also takes time. It's not a linear process. It will require trust, acceptance, and patience. You will have to accept the fact that you can't control the pace. You'll need to cultivate self-compassion and trust the process. It will also help if you learn to celebrate small victories, breathe through setbacks, and try not to be discouraged by moments of difficulty.

THE POWER OF HONESTY

Honesty is your ally on this journey. It's the tool you'll use to break down the walls you've built to protect yourself from the pain and trauma of your experiences. Being honest with yourself and others about your mental and emotional health is a fundamental step toward healing.

Therapists, counselors, mentors, program facilitators, peer support groups, and mental health professionals are trained to guide you through the process of healing and growth. They provide a safe space for you to explore your thoughts and feelings, helping you develop strategies to cope with stress, manage emotions, and overcome the challenges that have accumulated over time. But they can only help you if you're honest with them, and with yourself.

THE IMPORTANCE
OF PERSEVERANCE

Healing, recovery, and growth are often marked by periods of discomfort, as you confront painful truths and make changes in your life. These moments are signs of progress, not regression. Embrace them as opportunities for transformation.

Throughout this book, I'm going to share with you some themes that emerged as I interviewed these warriors. A prominent theme they all agree on is that healing is not a one-and-done project. It takes commitment, time, patience, and maintenance.

Maybe you've heard stories of a friend who went to therapy and is fine now, or a coworker who attended a treatment program and is doing great. While those things might be true, don't operate on the false assumption that any one thing fixed a person, or that it was easy.

That's not how healing works.

First of all, there is nothing that will magically fix you. This will be a collaborative effort. Healing programs, therapists, mentors, peers, and facilitators are there to help you learn new ways of being and develop skills and tools that will support your process of healing. You have to accept the help, do the work, and apply your new skills in order to maintain the progress you make.

There will be setbacks, and that's okay. Accept what happened, learn from it, give yourself grace, and when you're ready and able, get back on track.

PART II

THE JOURNEY

YOUR FELLOW TRAVELERS

—

In the next several chapters, you're going to meet warriors who are walking the path of healing. Nothing will make you feel validated and understood more than reading the stories of these people who are your true peers. No matter where you are on your life path, at least one of them has been there. No matter how messed up, or broken, or weak, or alone you have felt or are feeling, at least one of them has felt exactly the same.

Warriors, maybe more than any other group of people I can think of, tend to feel as though nobody truly understands what they've been through. If you feel that way, you aren't alone, and I agree with you. The warriors, protectors, guardians, and healers in this world encounter, deal with, witness, and endure the worst of humanity. The average person has no idea how much suffering, violence, abuse, sadness, pain, destruction, devastation, and death our warriors encounter over the course of a career.

But your peers know. There is nothing you could tell any of the people in this book that would surprise them or make them think less of you. You could sit in a room with these people and pour out all of your pain, shame, and dysfunction, and not one of them would judge you. They would hold space for you, and they would do anything in their power to help you find a way to heal.

This is the magic that happens when warriors support each other. First, you have to find the courage to let down your guard and open your mind and heart. Then, you start accepting help and support. You give yourself grace and allow yourself as much time as you need to heal. And then, somewhere down the road, your healing journey can serve as a beacon of hope to others.

I see this happening in so many different ways. I see the power of camaraderie, vulnerability, and storytelling beginning to transform the warrior world from one of silent suffering and false bravado to one of connecting, understanding, and healing. I see warriors allowing themselves and other warriors to express their feelings and admit to their frailties. I see warriors embracing their humanness, healing their hearts, and mending their relationships. I see people who once wanted to die, now wanting to live and help others find their way to healing.

Since my first book was published, I've heard from countless people who felt a connection with the nine warriors I interviewed for that book. Many have reported feeling seen, understood, and validated after reading those stories. The stories helped them feel less alone. Many have also reported feeling inspired by those nine people to make changes in their own lives. So, I knew it was important to stick with a similar format in this book.

In total, I spoke with fourteen people for the book you're reading now. Each has a compelling personal story, and every one of them shared their story openly and honestly. You'll feel that openness. You'll sense the vulnerability they had to embrace in order to let us in to their world. I also believe you'll realize you're not alone, and I hope you'll feel inspired to take a leap of faith and make some changes in your own life.

CHAPTER 6

#

Law Enforcement

———

I'm going to spend a little time setting up Keith's interview. I met Keith at an in-person training, and he turned out to be the inspiration for an enhanced version of my first book, *Mindfulness for Warriors,* which was recently rereleased as *The Mindfulness for Warriors Handbook.* If you've read that book, you've already read Keith's story in the preface. If you haven't, let me bring you up to speed.

In December of 2022, I attended my publishing company's annual holiday get-together online. This is an opportunity for fellow authors, my editor/publisher Brenda Knight, and others from Mango Publishing to come together, share, and celebrate.

Our facilitator kicked off the festivities by asking everyone to tell a positive story about their book, their year, or whatever they felt like sharing with the group. I decided to talk about something I had experienced just a few days earlier.

On the Saturday before this holiday celebration, three fellow Pause First Academy instructors and I had presented a full day of training for first responder retirees and those who anticipate retiring in five or so years. The workshop, *Navigating Retirement: Creating a Path to Purpose, Fulfillment, and Well-Being,* is intended to help people plan for and process the mental and emotional aspects of retirement.

During a break, a man approached me with my book in his hand, and I was not prepared for what he was about to say. "Your book saved my life," he said.

I was caught off guard, and I wasn't sure how to respond. Tears filled his eyes as he continued, "I had a suicide plan, and I was ready to execute that plan. And then your book came onto my path, and I changed my mind." Although I'll never get used to hearing those words, it wasn't the first time I'd heard them, and I am overcome with humility and gratitude every time.

I take my work very seriously, because I have come to know how many people across first responder professions are suffering due to the weight of the work, and I know all too well from my own experience how bad things can get when people refuse to, or aren't afforded the opportunity to, deal with the crushing pressure of that weight.

The sharing of my workshop story sparked a new level of interest within my publishing company. In the early months of the following year, they gave me the green light for a second book, and decided to retitle, enhance, and rerelease *Mindfulness for Warriors* under a new program called *Books that Save Lives*.

I am grateful to Keith for inspiring both projects; I'm happy to know him, and I'm really glad he's still here with us.

Thank you, Keith. Your story will inspire countless others. And one more thing. I appreciate your kind words about my book, but I want to be very clear about something. My book did not save your life. It sparked something inside you, yes. Most of that credit goes to the nine first responders and veterans who shared their stories in that book. But *you* made the difficult choices. *You* asked for help. *You* did the hard work, and you alone get credit for that, my friend.

Now, on to Keith's story.

Keith and I met for this interview via Zoom, and we spoke for around two hours. Our conversation was deep, real, and raw. He was open and honest, and allowed himself to be vulnerable. I was moved to tears and goose bumps during portions of our chat. Here's what I learned about Keith and his over-thirty-year career as a first responder.

First of all, he was a single dad. He raised his only daughter by himself, while also dealing with the intense demands of a law enforcement career. During his darkest times, his relationship with his daughter suffered, and the two were estranged for a period of time.

DIFFICULT EXPERIENCES

Keith ticked off a list of the usual difficult experiences most police officers endure, then moved pretty quickly to an event that occurred very early on and sort of hung over the rest of his career.

While Keith was in the police academy, he was involved in a shooting during a ride-along with a veteran officer. They attempted to stop a suspicious vehicle, which led to a car chase. As they pursued the car, the rider in the passenger seat began shooting at the police car through the back window.

At some point, the car stopped. The shooter jumped out of the car and ran. The duty officer engaged in a foot chase, leaving Keith behind with the other occupant of the car. Keith remembers the shooter pointing his gun directly at him and firing as he fled, but the gun didn't discharge. Keith was shocked that he wasn't hit during all of the shooting.

He was in full academy uniform and was wearing body armor, but because he was a recruit, he wasn't allowed to carry a gun. He wasn't sure what to do without a firearm to protect himself, so he got in position behind the door of the police car, acting as if he was holding a gun. He ordered the guy to the ground, then approached him and held him down, waiting for backup, which thankfully arrived.

While he was alone with the passenger, he heard more shots fired. He later learned that the suspect had been shot by the other officer, but didn't die.

As the police officers secured the scene, Keith was placed in a police car alone, for what felt like a very long time. After that, he was taken to headquarters, where he was interviewed by detectives. He remembers feeling scared and confused, like maybe he was in trouble or might be facing dismissal. He wasn't released to go home until late into the night, and he had to report to the academy early the next morning.

The next day at the academy, the recruits were going through scenarios—roleplaying to test decision-making and response to situations they might encounter on the job.

Afterwards, Keith was jotting down notes, completing an after-action report, and one of the academy trainers noticed his hands were shaking. The trainer asked him if he was shaken up by roleplaying and Keith said no, he wasn't sure why his hands were shaking. He told the instructor that he had been in a shooting the night before while on a ride-along, and he hadn't had much sleep. (Flash forward to the present: Keith now realizes he was experiencing physical symptoms caused by the traumatic experiences of the night before.)

Keith's shaking hands and mention of the shooting led to an immediate academy investigation. The next thing he knew, he was in a room by himself, where he had been asked to write a detailed report recounting his experience the night before. Once again, he felt worried that he was in some kind of trouble or that he might lose his job.

Ultimately, he did not get in trouble, nor was he dismissed. But that experience, and the surrounding emotion, fear, worry, and trauma, stuck with him throughout his career. He didn't dwell on these things, but he realizes now, they were always there.

Keith witnessed two other shootings early in his career, another officer-involved and one accidental shooting that occurred during a training exercise.

TURNING POINT

Keith's turning point came late in his career when he was working as a fire investigator. He started to notice he was losing the ability to emotionally disengage from cases. He felt that the hard outer shell that had allowed him to conduct the investigations dispassionately was no longer there to protect him from the emotions of the work.

His point of no return was initiated by a particularly difficult fire investigation involving twin babies that had died in a home fire. Keith determined that one baby had died of smoke inhalation, and the other had burned to death, and this realization hit him hard. He became extremely emotional over this case, and it haunted him like nothing before.

Keith says that's when he started to experience symptoms of severe trauma, although he didn't know much about trauma at the time. For whatever reason, that case opened a Pandora's box of feelings, memories, and images. Things from the past started coming up. He experienced terrible nightmares, and many sleepless nights, and would sometimes go three to four days at a time without any sleep.

He began drinking heavily and drinking himself to sleep every night. He remembers episodes of uncontrollable crying while in his police car. He was losing his tolerance of citizens, and his behavior, actions, and drinking started to push his now adult daughter away, which led to an estrangement.

It was during this time that Keith decided he didn't want to live anymore, so he set about getting his affairs order to ensure that everything he owned would go to his daughter.

During the course of planning his suicide, Keith heard about an organization called The Battle Within, a five-day retreat in nature for first responders and veterans struggling with anxiety, depression, post-traumatic stress, or a diagnosis of PTSD (post-traumatic stress disorder). He applied for the program, and the prospect of possibly getting help gave him a small glimmer of hope. He temporarily put his suicide plan on hold. He thought, *I'll try this, and if it helps, maybe I won't kill myself.*

But this happened at the height of COVID, and he wasn't able to get the days off work to attend the program. However, one of the members of The Battle Within staff sent him a copy of my book, *Mindfulness for Warriors*.

Keith started reading the book immediately, and says he remembers crying because he no longer felt alone. The book helped him realize that others have felt the way he had been feeling. He connected strongly with the first responders and veterans and their stories.

As a result of reading the book, Keith says, he quit drinking alcohol, started experimenting with mindfulness, and put his suicide plans on hold.

Next, his daughter started to come back around, which solidified his decision not to kill himself. He also decided to get professional help.

At first, Keith tried to hide the fact that he was in therapy from his employer. But when his therapist recommended that he seek more targeted and in-depth help from a local inpatient program for veterans and first responders with PTSD, he knew he would have to make his employer aware. He did so, and then immersed himself in the program, and completed the outpatient follow-up as well.

Keith says he felt supported by his employer when he was honest about his situation and attended the program. But he also felt somewhat isolated.

He is now retired. He admits to feeling sad when he left the job. But, looking back, he knows it was the right thing to do. He says retirement saved his life, and he knows it will also extend his life.

Keith has strong advice for anyone in a similar position who will listen:

"Don't wait. I waited too long, and it almost cost me my life. If you don't want your employer to know, then go get help on your own. But don't wait and let this ruin your life, because it will."

For those of you who are wondering, because I sure was, Keith and his daughter did reconcile. He's been honest with her about his struggles and his path to healing, which has helped them work on rebuilding and redefining their relationship.

TOOLS

Tools Keith has found most helpful:

- Mindfulness

- Counseling

- EMDR (Eye Movement Desensitization and Reprocessing) therapy[1]

- Writing and journaling

---

1 As a side note, Keith points out that it's crucial to find a therapist who specializes in first responder trauma and PTSD, both for counseling and EMDR therapy.

WHAT NEEDS TO CHANGE

Keith was quick to answer: "Let the stigma go." While he admits to sometimes still feeling a little embarrassed, he remembers that, prior to seeking help, he felt that asking for help was a sign of weakness, a signal he couldn't handle the job, and that he'd be viewed as a loser if he sought help.

Now, he realizes that is all part of the stigma that prevents first responders from seeking life-saving assistance with their job-related trauma.

As part of his "don't wait" message, Keith goes on to say, "First responders must be encouraged to address the trauma at the time they experience it. Trying to ignore the symptoms or hold in the emotions will not work. The memories, images, and feelings *will* resurface. So, people have to deal with them and process them when they happen."

"Think of it this way," he continues, "you're not going to keep running on a sprained ankle, you're going to get it looked at. You should deal with mental and emotional wounds in the same way."

Keith remains focused on healing, and still attends counseling sessions. He practices mindfulness, and uses writing and journaling to help him process difficult things. He hasn't figured out what's next for him in life, so for now, he does a lot of volunteer work, and continues to work on himself.

CHAPTER 7

ASHLEY

Law Enforcement

I met Ashley through my work with CIT (Crisis Intervention Team). She's the CIT sergeant for a large local metropolitan police department. Ashley has a big, positive personality and she's just really likeable. She has quite a history and quite a story, and I'm so grateful she agreed to talk to me for this book.

Like many other warriors I've talked to over many years, Ashley had a rough childhood. Childhood trauma is fairly prevalent among veterans and first responders. As I discuss in more detail in William's interview, coming up next, there's a simple ten-question Adverse Childhood Experiences (ACE) test you can take if you'd like to see your score and find out what it means.

The bottom line is, adverse childhood experiences can impact your adult life in detrimental ways, but awareness of this can help you face things, heal, and overcome the damage. Most importantly, dealing with it can help prevent you from repeating the patterns with your own children.

Unfortunately, I've met a lot of people in these professions who have poor or even nonexistent relationships with their children. I've also received emails from adult children of warriors who have shared their stories of difficult, unhappy childhoods, and how that pain plagues them even in adulthood.

I know this is an uncomfortable topic for some, and that a lot of people would rather not talk about it, or think about, and just move on. The problem with that is, childhood abuse and neglect can affect your life and inform your choices in ways you're not conscious of. But the chain of pain can be broken with the proper interventions and support. This is yet another reason why I am a huge proponent of therapy.

It's important to note that most children who are abused or neglected are like fish in water, meaning it's all they know. This will be highlighted in Ashley's story, and if you experienced a dysfunctional childhood, maybe it will help you determine if addressing your past might help you function more healthfully as an adult.

DIFFICULT EXPERIENCES

ADVERSE CHILDHOOD EXPERIENCES

Ashley says she has experienced more personal life trauma than job-related trauma. She describes her childhood as negative, dysfunctional, and traumatic. She had a very absent mother who was married seven times and was both neglectful and abusive. Ashley was forced to be the "adult" in the household, and as a result, she became hyper-independent, something she still grapples with today. She also felt overly responsible at a very young age, not only for herself, but for everyone and everything around her, another issue she's still working through.

Hyper-independence is similar to hypervigilance. The prefix "hyper" signifies over, above, high, excessive, and above normal. It is not *hyper*vigilance that keep you alive, it's vigilance. And it's not *hyper*-independence that makes you self-sufficient, it's independence. When vigilance and independence become hyper, they cause problems and can wreak havoc on your health and your life.

Hyper-responsibility, also known as an inflated sense of responsibility or hyper-responsibility syndrome, is often rooted in childhood. It's a belief or a cognitive bias by which a person feels they are personally responsible for people and events outside of their control.

Is it any wonder that a person suffering from hyper-responsibility would become a first responder or would choose to join the military? Of course not. Their sense of responsibility is so profound that they feel responsible for protecting, guarding, or saving entire communities, or their whole country. I have so much love and respect for the people who step into these roles, but it gives me a heavy heart to know the burden that hyper-responsibility places on them.

One time, when Ashley was around twelve or thirteen, her mother attempted suicide and Ashley was the one who found her. After this incident, Ashley called a local psychiatric hospital to try and get help for her mother. They told her that her mother was an adult and would have to call them herself, which, of course, she was not going to do. Let this sink in: Ashley was a child trying to get psychiatric help for her parent. This story breaks my heart.

In high school, Ashley was an elite athlete and received multiple college scholarship offers. She was looking forward to escaping her life circumstances and getting an education so she could build a successful life on her own. But all of that disappeared when her beloved and treasured grandfather passed away. He was really all Ashley had, and his death devastated her. She quit playing sports and started partying. The loss of the only solid adult in her life derailed her plans and robbed her of opportunities.

Right after high school, instead of going off to college on an athletic scholarship, Ashley got her own apartment, worked nonstop, and took college classes part-time on the side.

Luckily, when she was a little older and working for a psychiatrist, someone suggested to her that she would be a good match for police work. Originally, that was a hard no for Ashley, but she agreed to take an aptitude test out of curiosity. And which career did she most align with? Police officer. So, she decided to apply, she got in, and the rest is history.

It wasn't until many years later, when Ashley was a full-grown adult and already a police officer, that she realized she had grown up witnessing domestic violence. It's like I said—fish don't know they're in water, or that there is something other than water. Water is all they know. If you experienced a dysfunctional childhood, you might not be aware of how much that has impacted your adult life. If that's the case, I hope Ashley's story will help you reflect, and maybe even take a step toward healing your past.

TURNING POINT

Ashley's first big turning point came when she attended a weeklong program for first responders and veterans. She says she only attended in order to get a friend of hers to go. At the time, Ashley didn't think she needed it herself. (I've heard that one before.)

But the program was a huge eye-opener for her. It prompted her to evaluate her marriage, among other things. Most importantly, the program helped her realize she needed to work on herself. So, she did just that, starting with regular therapy appointments.

Once she began working on herself and digging into things from her childhood and past, Ashley decided to end her marriage. She doesn't speak ill of her ex-husband; in fact, she says he's a great guy. What she realized was that she didn't love *herself*. Therefore, she couldn't fathom how her husband could truly love her.

Ashley became aware that her painful childhood had led her to make poor decisions when choosing partners, but her ex-husband was different—he had grown up in a much more stable environment, and she couldn't believe he loved her the way he professed to, when she felt so broken inside.

The year Ashley got divorced, she was feeling pretty good about her progress. She was in therapy, on a healing path, committed to being a good mother and role model to her children, and ready for what was next for her in life. But later that same year, Ashley encountered a massive setback.

SETBACK

On Sunday, October 1, 2017, Ashley was in Las Vegas, celebrating her best friend's fortieth birthday at a Jason Aldean concert. As I'm sure you know, there was a mass shooting during that concert.

This is a critical part of Ashley's story, and it connects to one of the main themes that have arisen from these interviews: *Healing is not a one-and-done.* You will have setbacks. Some will be minor; some will be more significant. The key to navigating these inevitable setbacks is to have a war chest full of wellness and resilience tools, skills, and support in place.

This birthday celebration-turned-nightmare was made worse by the fact that both women are cops. Both have been trained in emergency response, active shooter preparedness, crowd control, and firearms use, and both are programmed to help, save, and rescue others. But in this situation, they felt helpless. There wasn't a damn thing they could do to help or to stop this nightmare.

They were not there as first responders. They weren't wearing body armor or carrying guns. They were tourists trying to have a little fun. This was their break from the world of emergencies and tragedies. And there they were, pinned down by an active shooter, and just trying to survive. They are both mothers. They have a lot to lose.

Luckily, both women escaped unharmed—physically. But the mental and emotional wounds from that awful experience will never fully heal. You don't live through something like that and then just forget about it.

Now, remember what I told you about Ashley's childhood and how it caused her to develop a propensity toward hyper-independence and hyper-responsibility? Well, guess what happened when she and her best friend were being shot at...hyper-responsibility instantly kicked in and flooded her system. She unintentionally defaulted right back to those old feelings.

During the event, she was flooded with thoughts and feelings of guilt and responsibility for what was happening. Going to Vegas and attending the concert were her ideas, so she felt like this was her fault; and now she had to figure out how to get them out of this, and how to save her friend's life.

Even after returning home, and long after the incident, she still carried the pain of being responsible for this happening to her friend. And she felt responsible for her friend's pain as well. It was debilitating, and in Ashley's words, "This event created a downward spiral for me. I reverted back to all of my old bad habits, and I felt like all of the work I had done on myself was out the window."

Ashley recalls spending several months in this spiral. Then, she had a wake-up call. She can't remember a specific day or reason for this, but she says she started to realize that she had a responsibility to her children, and that she needed to get ahold of herself and put her kids first.

Fortunately, she was able to do so. Getting focused on her children and recommitting to being a good mom and role model for them was the motivation Ashley needed to regroup and get back to self-care and good daily habits.

She says this journey hasn't been perfect and she has experienced other, albeit less severe, setbacks. But she hasn't gone backward, and she doesn't intend to. She is determined to never become any version of her mother.

Still a single mom, Ashley continues to work on herself and focus on her kids. She's learning to accept herself, and she has stopped looking for partners who need to be saved or rescued. She's moving forward, using the tools she's gained over the years, and focusing on her well-being.

Ashley is a shining example of a warrior who has been through the darkest of days but keeps moving toward the light. Her story of tragedy and triumph is inspiring, and I'm so grateful to her for sharing her story with us.

TOOLS

Here are the tools Ashley has found most helpful on her wellness journey:

- Therapy

- Meditation

    * Ashley credits meditation as a huge game-changer for her. She has been diagnosed with ADHD and describes her mind as "going a million miles a minute." But she trained herself to meditate, and now she relies heavily on meditation as a wellness practice. She says she definitely notices a difference when she skips it.

- Exercise

- Having the right people around her

WHAT NEEDS TO CHANGE

First, Ashley talked about the importance of a mindset shift in the first responder world. She believes people need to understand that our brains weren't created to handle intense and prolonged stress and trauma. So, first responders—and this applies to active military and veterans too, obviously—need to be allowed to take care of their mental health. Also, she says it will help when more people start being honest and open about their struggles.

She also points to the importance of leadership embracing and supporting this movement toward supporting mental health, and she highlights the significance of eliminating the stigma around this. She says job-related mental health issues are common in these professions and people shouldn't be made to feel bad when they need help.

And lastly, she feels there need to be more warrior-specific programs that aren't in any way attached to the organization the individual works for.

CHAPTER 8

WILLIAM

United States Air Force Veteran

———

I met William through my work with The Battle Within. He completed that program, and then became a mentor. We chatted from time to time at the cohorts, and then we met for coffee to talk about meditation and other things.

A while back, he agreed to a really interesting podcast-style interview with me, which you can find on the Pause First Academy YouTube channel. The title of that "Pausecast," as we call them, is "Transformation," with the subtitle, "cold, hard, angry." After reading William's story, you're probably going to want to go watch that.

William is quiet, kind, polite, and intelligent. He's a fascinating person to talk to because he's multi-faceted and multi-talented. He's a creative, a philosopher, and just a really decent guy.

At the onset of our conversation for this book, we talked about childhood trauma. William says he feels like 90 percent of veterans he has met experienced childhood trauma. That honestly caught me off guard, but I will say, I have met and worked with a lot of warriors who admit to experiencing trauma as a kid, and many don't realize the impact that can have on us as adults.

As I touched on in Ashley's section, there is something called the ACE (Adverse Childhood Experiences) test. It's a questionnaire that asks about traumatic experiences that took place early in your life. It provides you with a score from 1–10. Higher ACE scores have been linked to challenges later in life, including physical and mental health problems. The ACE test is not a diagnostic tool, but it can serve as a guide to help you better understand how a difficult childhood might be impacting your adult life.

A lot of people who work in helping or service-oriented professions were motivated to do so because of childhood experiences. Sometimes it's because they had a bad experience with law enforcement, social services, or some other entity, and they want others to have a better experience. Other times, people who had a positive experience with someone in the military, a firefighter, or a medical professional, want to follow in their footsteps and offer the same care or service to others. Another aspect William pointed out was how many people he's met who joined the military just to escape their home situation. I, too, have spoken with many veterans who say they joined the military to break free from dysfunctional childhood homes.

In our Pause First Academy workshops, we often talk about the ACE test, and depending on the group, sometimes we have them go through the questionnaire during the presentation. We don't want to upset or traumatize anyone in our classes, but we feel it's important for people who work in these challenging professions to understand the effects that childhood trauma can have on us as adults. Our hope is that making folks aware of this fact might inspire them to address it in some meaningful way that brings them a better understanding of themselves, but also, relief. Unconscious, untreated trauma can wreak havoc on our lives.

You can easily find a free ACE test online if you're curious, and as I mentioned in Ashley's section, you can learn more about ACEs by visiting the CDC website (www.cdc.gov) or the National Alliance on Mental Illness (NAMI) website (www.nami.org).

William says he definitely experienced childhood trauma, and feels it impacts him more than job-related stress and trauma. The military stuff, he says, he can reflect on without the same level of heaviness as the childhood memories.

William joined the Air Force at the age of twenty-one. His girlfriend (now wife) was pregnant, and he says he needed some direction in life and the ability to take care of a family. Military life was difficult for him at first because he considers himself to be oppositional-defiant, so authority and discipline were challenging for him.

DIFFICULT EXPERIENCES

In 2001, William was sent to Afghanistan, about one month after 9/11 happened. The military hadn't gotten organized over there yet, so when he arrived, he says it felt like the Wild West.

Looking back, William says he was not in any way prepared for being in a combat zone, nor was he prepared for dealing with the violence. He had been trained in aircraft repair initially, and eventually cross-trained into air traffic control, not combat.

Immediately upon arrival, he was repairing planes during military conflict, under occasional gunfire and frequent rocket attacks. On top of this, during later deployments as an air traffic controller, his facility was right next to the morgue, which was a stark and constant reminder of where he was and what was happening around him.

After leaving the military, William became a civilian contractor for air traffic control in Afghanistan and did that job for over a year. Part of the job involved authorizing air-space clearances for unmanned drone strikes, something he has wrestled with ever since.

While he was working as a civilian contractor in Afghanistan, William watched a movie called *Gandhi*. This is a biographical film based on the life of Mahatma Gandhi. Gandhi was an international public figure who espoused the spiritual principles of equality, tolerance, and nonviolence. William remembers being hesitant to watch it at first, because it wasn't the type of movie he would typically be interested in.

But there wasn't much to do over there, and there weren't a lot of movies to choose from, so he watched it. The movie introduced William to the concepts of peace and nonviolence, ideas that were foreign to him at the time. He says this is definitely what inspired him to start thinking about war and death in a new and different way, and after watching the movie, he took his first step onto a path of spiritual exploration.

As part of that exploration, William started to think about what he was doing—taking large sums of money to be complicit in death became untenable for him. So, he decided to get out of that line of work.

TURNING POINT

When William returned home from his contracting job, he says he was not in good shape. He remembers an incident within his first day or two of being home in which he was standing, looking out of a window, and his wife walked up behind him to give him a hug. He started crying, but he distinctly remembers he really didn't feel anything, or at least he didn't feel what you would expect a person to feel as a result of a loving touch from their spouse. In fact, he remembers feeling dead inside.

Alarm bells started going off. He knew something was wrong. At first, he turned to alcohol to deal with his issues. Sound familiar? If so, you're not alone. This is an all-too-common go-to for warriors, and it never leads to a good place.

Next, he enrolled in art school, but says he was just going through the motions. He didn't feel passionate or enthusiastic about it. At one point, the students were encouraged to explore their feelings. He complied with the instructions, but quickly realized he didn't have the right tools in place to do this, and he fell apart emotionally.

In his senior year, he had what he describes as a nervous breakdown, and checked himself into the VA for inpatient psychiatric treatment. He says the VA was a start, but not exactly helpful. He does, however, credit his time in VA care for preventing him from taking his own life.

William says suicidal ideation has been a part of his life since childhood and throughout his teen years, and he admits he still wrestles with it sometimes. He recalls thoughts of suicide being intense when he first came back from Afghanistan. He knows now that when he felt like that, he didn't really want to die, he just wanted the suffering to end.

After the VA, he began trying various forms of therapy. One therapist recommended yoga and meditation. He was hesitant at first and says it took him a couple of years to consider trying these modalities, and more like four to five years before he fully embraced them.

He remembers that when he finally fully committed to sit and stay in meditation, it was so impactful that he decided to keep doing it. This led to a very deep and rich meditation practice. He started reading books and studying meditation. Now meditation is his number one well-being tool. He admits he sometimes gets away from regular practice, but he always comes back to it.

TOOLS

- Meditation—William points out that the ability to meditate is one thing, and the ability to sit and do it regularly is quite another. And, he says, practicing meditation consistently is what makes the practice powerful.

- Reading self-help-type material—He sought out self-improvement books that appealed to him, especially those that support a meditation practice.

- Talking—Being vulnerable with people is difficult for him, but he knows it's important.

- Listening—Active listening. William defines active listening as a skill, and he places it right up there with meditation. He started by reading books about how to develop listening skills. He focuses on being an active listener whenever someone opens up to him. He says being a good active listener requires your attention, and he adds, there's no better way to develop discipline around attention than to practice meditation. He's certain that cultivating these skills has made him a better husband, dad, and friend.

- A creative outlet—William believes everyone needs some type of creative outlet and he says everyone is creative, whether they realize it or not.

- Writing/Journaling—He calls his writing practice "morning pages." Every morning he brain-dumps onto the page. There are no rules, he just writes.

He wraps up this part of our conversation by emphasizing that, with all of these tools, you have to *do* them. You have to put them into practice and use them consistently in order to reap the benefits. Reading a book and feeling that you have somehow changed is an insufficient strategy to create deep, lasting change.

And finally, he advises that healing is not a one-and-done. There will not be one single thing that you do one time that's going to fix everything. It's a process, a journey.

He says that first, you need to accept that the trauma and mental and emotional injury is part of you. It will help if you can stop thinking of it as something you need to get rid of or fix, and instead view it as something you have to learn to work with. And he adds, "Don't beat yourself up for feeling what you're feeling."

He goes on to say that facing it and accepting it doesn't mean you have to deal with it at this heavy level forever. In fact, facing it actually helps lighten the load of it. "Give yourself grace," he encourages. "Give yourself time."

William admits he has setbacks. He's not always great. He says when he experiences a setback, he focuses on giving himself space and latitude to work through it. He goes on to say that you can expect good times and bad times, so focus on learning the new tools and skills, and be diligent about applying them. However, he also notes that even these tools will not always appeal to you, nor will they work all the time. "But" he says, "everything around this becomes easier when you allow yourself mercy, grace, time, and space to work the program. You just keep working through things."

As a former weightlifter and bodybuilder, William uses a gym analogy to make his point. He says, "It's like building muscle. The image in your mirror does not change day to day. You just have to trust and have faith that you will get to where you want to be. You keep showing up to the gym, no matter what. And in healing, you keep showing up for yourself."

Well said, William. That is a clear and powerful analogy, and one I think will resonate with a lot of people.

WHAT NEEDS TO CHANGE

The first thing William brought up is something he says is prevalent among military veterans. It has to do with frontline people minimizing the experiences of, and complaining about the support given to, non-frontline, non-direct-combat people. He feels this needs to change because you do not have to be on the front lines of combat to be negatively impacted by military service.

He also notes that non-frontline people need to stop feeling as if they are not worthy of or don't deserve the same level of care, empathy, programs, and support provided to combat veterans who were engaged in direct, active combat.

CHAPTER 9

RANDY

Firefighter/Medic

———

Randy found my first book, *Mindfulness for Warriors*, through an online search. After reading the book, he connected with me and Pause First Academy. He first reached out back in 2020. Over the years we've messaged here and there, and he has participated in online training, purchased a PFA membership, and even won a prize in one of our prize drawings!

After chatting back and forth for a few years, I got curious about Randy's work experiences and his desire to focus on self-care and well-being. So, as I was planning my interviews for this book, I took a chance and reached out to him. He was immediately open to speaking with me, for which I am grateful.

Randy and I met over Zoom and had a lengthy, interesting, and at times, sobering conversation. I'm always awestruck and humbled by my conversations with these folks, and this was no exception. He's a twenty-two-year veteran of fire and EMS who is retired, but he's still a peer support specialist and is a huge proponent of responder peer support and mental health. I have a feeling Randy's work in the warrior world isn't finished yet. I think it'll just look a little different in the future.

DIFFICULT EXPERIENCES

When I asked Randy to tell me about some of the difficult experiences he encountered on the job, he told me there is a series of calls that remain in his psyche, and probably always will. "The heaviest calls," he shared, "were always the ones involving children."

He started by describing the first child-involved call he encountered in his career. The child was around two and a half years old, was experiencing complications from an earlier surgery, and was not breathing when medics arrived. Randy vividly remembers working on that child and not being able to bring him back. At the time, Randy had an infant son at home, so this call hit him very hard. He remembers arriving home after that shift, seeing his own son, and breaking down, totally overwhelmed by emotion. This was the first heavy brick in the trauma backpack he ended up carrying around for years.

Another child-involved call that sticks in his mind is an unresponsive woman and her baby, who was crawling and climbing on her mother's motionless body when Randy's team arrived. They were unable to revive the woman, leaving the baby motherless. This is one of the images Randy can't erase from his head. "Calls like this," he said, "will always be with me."

Aside from tragedies involving kids, Randy cites the influx of drug overdoses as another heavy brick in his invisible trauma backpack.

On one particular shift, Randy remembers a guy overdosing and being very close to death. The medics were able to bring him back, and they transported him to the hospital to recover. Later *that same day, on that same shift*, Randy's unit got a call on *that same person*. Another overdose, and this time, the man did not survive.

Randy remembers thinking about the person and asking, "Did I care more about your life than you did?" and says he felt numb after those two calls.

He goes on to say how traumatic scenes, like the ones he has described here, have always been a part of the work, but nobody talks about the incidents in any meaningful way. After especially difficult calls, he remembers having thoughts like, "Are we just supposed to go back to the station? Carry on? Go to bed and *sleep*? We're supposed to sleep after something like that? And then just go to the next call?"

Unfortunately for first responders, the answer is, yes.

PANIC ATTACK

I wanted to share the story of Randy's first panic attack, although at the time, he didn't know what was happening to him. Over the years, I've talked to a lot of people who say they didn't know what was happening the first time they experienced debilitating anxiety, a panic attack, or a bout of depression. And because the symptoms can be so scary, shocking, and overwhelming, people sometimes feel confused or embarrassed, and will therefore keep these events to themselves, until they become nearly incapacitated and have no choice but to reach out for help.

Randy remembers being on a ladder with his air mask on. The mask was working fine, but out of the blue, he started to feel intensely as if he couldn't breathe. It was so bad that he had no choice but to tell his lieutenant he needed to come down because he was struggling to breathe. At the time, that was an extremely difficult and disorienting experience. But later on, Randy learned that what he experienced that day was a panic attack. As he learned more about trauma and the body's response to trauma, Randy was able to make sense of those experiences and understand how and why they happened.

THE BEGINNING OF THE END

While working at the scene of a very large structure fire, Randy found himself on an upper floor of the burning building, searching for people, when suddenly everything froze. He said it was like time stood still. He was in total blackness, had zero visibility, and the world around him went completely silent. He felt like he was in some weird bubble, closed off from the world.

He remembers thinking, "I'm all alone, above a fire. Does anyone even know where I am? I don't want to die." In that moment, Randy found himself thinking about his family. The backpack was getting heavier.

He recalls this as being one of the strangest experiences he's ever had. It instigated conversations with his wife and a therapist, which led him to make the decision to leave the profession.

TURNING POINT

While still on the job, Randy heard about a mental health symposium being presented by his state's fire academy, and he registered for it. Attending this event, he says, was his turning point. He describes it as a breakthrough, because he learned about mental health-related issues he had never considered, became interested in wellness, and was introduced to the power of peer support.

After attending this symposium, Randy took the steps to get educated and certified as a peer support specialist, and he helped pioneer peer support for fire service in his home state.

Not long after this, he learned about a program called Frontline Frontiers, and began recommending the program to coworkers and colleagues. One day, Randy realized that he probably needed to walk his talk and attend the program himself. So he signed up.

Frontline Frontiers was a two-week, outpatient, resilience-based program for first responders. Randy says he learned so much and really got a lot out of that program. He felt different after attending and remembers his son commenting on the big changes he noticed as well.

Completing this program inspired Randy to become passionate about mental health and wellness. He reports learning about trauma and secondary trauma, and how gaining that knowledge led to everything starting to make sense. He had a much better understanding of what he had endured on the job, and how it had impacted him mentally, emotionally, and physically. These epiphanies helped him heal, and ultimately helped him make the decision to retire.

TOOLS

Here is the list of tools Randy says have helped him on his journey to health and well-being:

- Books

- Mindfulness

- Journaling

- Therapy

- Wellness apps/guided meditations

- Staying active/fitness

- Being in nature

WHAT NEEDS TO CHANGE

Randy believes that the culture needs to embrace the fact that first responders need outlets and tools readily available to help them deal with and process the things that impact them on the job. He says this should include education, training, and on-site resources.

One crucial point he makes is that too often, these organizations wait until there is a crisis before they deal with things. Randy says instead, they need to offer tools and skills along the way to help people prepare mentally and emotionally for the crises before they occur. Then, there should be protocols in place to offer support swiftly and adequately when there is a critical incident.

I asked him what the barriers are that might prevent people from reaching out for help. He said, "People are afraid of vulnerability because they've been taught to take care of others and neutralize their own feelings. So, use of the resources has to be strongly embraced and supported by the top person or people." He acknowledged that is not always the case, and that a "changing of the guard" will help, when some of the older, more set-in-their-ways people begin to retire.

Before we wrapped up our conversation, Randy shared something I feel is important to note. He said after he made the decision to retire, he kind of felt like hiding for a while. He said he felt a little weak. But he assured me he longer feels like that. He's done a lot of work on his own well-being, and he knows he did the best thing for himself, his life, and his family.

Why did I feel this was important to include? Because I know a lot of you have been afraid to appear weak, and maybe that has prevented you from asking for help. The act of seeking help is not a sign of weakness.

In fact, it just might be the thing that saves your relationships, your family, or maybe even your life.

CHAPTER 10

DARREN

Law Enforcement | Air Force Veteran

On one of the last pages of my first book, *Mindfulness for Warriors*, there's a line that reads, "And finally, thank you, Darren Ivey, for giving me a shot."

I'd like to introduce you to Darren. In 2017, when I was making phone calls and begging for meetings and trying to get someone to let me teach cops how to meditate, Darren took my call and agreed to a meeting. He listened, he understood what I was trying to do, and he said yes. I'll always credit him with giving me my big break into this world.

Back then, Darren was a police commander at a local agency. He had been teaching a block of training called Building Resilience, Surviving Secondary Trauma. That course was created by a group of people from Darren's police department, along with a group of people from a local behavioral health center. It was originally intended for law enforcement, but because the curriculum translated easily across professions, they ended up offering it to all first responders and others working in adjacent occupations.

When Darren and I initially met, he told me that in the Building Resilience training, they touched on mindfulness, but they wanted to add more because it was a popular topic. So, he told me to put together a training and let me tag along with him to an all-day conference, where he graciously debuted and allowed me to present

"An Introduction to Meditation and Mindfulness" to a room full of law enforcement professionals. And that was my start!

I went on to become a certified instructor of the Building Resilience course, and Darren became a Pause First Academy trainer. We've worked together a lot over the years, collaborating, designing curriculum, tag-team teaching, and co-facilitating. And we've become friends.

Around here, we call Darren the Godfather of Resilience. (And when he's not in the room, we call him the *grandfather* of resilience.) Ha!

Darren began his career in law enforcement as a military police officer in the United States Air Force, which he joined at the age of eighteen. When he was twenty-seven, he left the military, and was hired by a large metropolitan police department. He says he always knew he wanted to be a police officer. He has a vivid memory of Officer Friendly visiting his elementary school, and he remembers thinking that was really cool. (Anybody remember Officer Friendly from back in the day? I do!) Darren also had a favorite uncle and a grandfather who were police officers, and he says as far back as he can remember, he was drawn to the profession.

I meet a lot of people in law enforcement, fire service, EMS, and the military who are self-proclaimed adrenaline junkies and thrill-seekers. Darren says that was not the case for him. He says he got into law enforcement because he had a sincere desire to help people.

Over the course of his nearly thirty-year career, Darren enjoyed many different roles. Early on, he was part of a community policing initiative that was designed to help officers get to know citizens and allow citizens to get to know and become comfortable with the officers. Each officer in this initiative was assigned to a particular neighborhood. He loved that work, and looking back, he says, it might be his favorite assignment of all time.

After that, Darren shifted to administration in the form of planning, research, and policy development. Then he was promoted to sergeant and went back to patrol.

Over the years, Darren also worked in Youth Services (Police Athletic League, DARE), Narcotics, and Diversity and Inclusion; he was the CIT coordinator, executive officer of the Administrative Bureau, and HR commander. He retired in December of 2021 at the rank of major.

DIFFICULT EXPERIENCES

Darren's first truly traumatizing experience in life happened well before he became a police officer. When he was just fourteen years old, his mother died of cancer. He says he didn't realize until much later in life just how much that loss impacted him.

During Darren's time as an MP in the Air Force, he was charged with investigating fatality accidents. Back then, he says, he had the ability to turn off his emotions so he could do that difficult work. Many years later, as Darren learned more and more about trauma, he began to connect some dots. He realized that, at the young age of fourteen, he had unconsciously turned off his emotions in order to survive the death of his mother.

In my years of working in the world of first responder trauma, I have learned that when we humans turn off an emotion in order to protect ourselves from pain, we simultaneously dull *all* of our emotions. In other words, we do not possess the ability to selectively disable a single emotion. Rather, we lose the ability to feel the depth and breadth of all of our emotions.

This is called emotional detachment, and it occurs when we knowingly or unknowingly turn off our connection to our emotions. Emotional detachment refers to a muting or a numbing of our feelings.

While it can serve as a form of protection, it can also lead to an inability to feel joy or happiness, difficulty maintaining healthy close personal relationships, and a diminished desire or ability to be loving and affectionate with our family.

If any of this rings true for you, please consider working with a mental health professional to address the issue and learn to reengage with your emotions in a healthy way.

Darren admits to making a lot of positive changes after learning about the effects of trauma. He discovered and put into practice wellness tools and resilience skills that helped him reconnect with his emotions and establish healthier relationships with the people he loves.

The first career-related trauma Darren recalls happened while he was in the Air Force. He remembers being on the flight line and watching an F-4 take off, when all of a sudden, the plane went belly-up and crashed. The pilot was able to eject, but was killed by the impact, and Darren saw the whole thing. He says this was the first incident in his law enforcement career that stuck in his psyche. He recalls having flashbacks and other symptoms, but there was no option except to carry on. So he did.

In another incident, a fellow Air Force MP was killed on train tracks and Darren was part of the team that helped with the investigation afterward. He knew the deceased officer was a father, and as a young father himself, this shook Darren to his core. He says that was the first time he connected the work he did with his personal life. This incident heightened his awareness of the fragility of life and the importance of being here for the people you love. This was amplified, no doubt, by the fact that he lost a parent when he was still a child.

Moving forward a few years to when Darren had completed the police academy, he was in the field training process, and was out with his FTO (Field Training Officer). An "assist the officer" call came in, and he and the FTO were the first ones on scene. When they arrived, the suspect had managed to wrest the officer's gun away from him and was on top of the officer, pointing the gun at his head.

The suspect saw the other officers pull up and fled. A foot chase ensued, and the officers were able to catch him. Luckily, nobody was shot or seriously injured.

Darren remembers the jarring feeling of seeing a police gun in the hand of a citizen. He says it was the first time he felt vulnerable. He had just witnessed, and was forced to face, the dangerous nature of his job and the real possibility of being injured or killed. The invincibility he had felt as a young military police officer was gone.

In terms of difficult experiences, Darren was quick to say, "Anything involving kids." He recounted seeing children living in poverty and filth, and finding children who had been abandoned in some of the worst living conditions you can imagine. He says it was heartbreaking caring for those kids until arrangements were made for them, and then handing them over to child services. "Those kids," he said, "stay with you."

He also noted that death notifications were some of the most difficult things he ever did in his career, and he talked about the mental and emotional toll of losing two of his own officers to suicide.

TURNING POINT

Darren's first turning point came when he embarked on the mission to create the resilience training I mentioned earlier. That project started when he was contacted by the COO of a local behavioral health center. She had some grant money and wanted to work with law enforcement professionals to create a trauma training specifically for their career field.

Working on that training course, learning about trauma and secondary trauma, and delivering the presentation to his peers were life-changing for Darren. It helped him identify some issues in his own life and make some needed changes.

Darren's next and most important turning point occurred in his own home. He recalls arriving home from work after a difficult shift, and getting upset with his son, who was five years old at the time. He says he remembers getting really mad, but he can't remember now what his son had done. He admits it was probably something small.

He started scolding his son, who was standing on the steps while Darren towered over him, angry and yelling. Darren says his son crouched down, put his hands over his ears, and started crying and screaming from fear. All of a sudden, Darren realized how out of control he was, and that his child was terrified of him. In that moment, he snapped out of it. He became aware of how he must look to his son; this big, angry figure, looming over him, yelling and enraged. After this experience, Darren says he made big adjustments to his parenting by focusing on some of the trauma-sensitive wellness skills and tools he had learned while creating the trauma training.

TOOLS

Here are the tools Darren has found most helpful on his journey to well-being:

- Talking. This is Darren's number one wellness tool because, he admits, he used to bottle things up and hold things in. His advice: talk about everything, talk about your emotions.

- Meditation. He was introduced to meditation when he attended the Save a Warrior program. They taught him a technique that made sense and worked for him.

- Mindfulness. He uses music as a mindful tool to bring himself into the moment and then carry him to a better place.

WHAT NEEDS TO CHANGE

Darren believes that wellness, resilience, and self-care need to be included and presented in the hiring process. He says organizations should let candidates know that their health and wellness, to include mental and emotional health, will be taken very seriously, and that it will be a part of their initial and ongoing training.

Then, this training needs to be included in the academy. Recruits should learn about trauma, understand what secondary trauma is, and discover ways to process trauma and protect their mental health. Additionally, he says this training should be ongoing and reinforced throughout their career.

He goes on to say that self-care has to become an expectation in first responder professions, and that top leaders must embrace and model this.

In Darren's opinion, wellness should be part of chief selection, and other leadership selection processes as well. He envisions candidates for promotion being asked, "What are your plans to promote and support health and wellness?" Then this becomes part of their evaluation process. Did they deliver on their promises?

He also says mental, emotional, and psychological health and wellness must become part of the core values of every organization.

One more thing. Darren wants you to know that it is never too late. He was twenty years into his law enforcement career before he learned about these things and started to make changes.

CHAPTER 11

JAMIE

Licensed Clinical Social Worker (LCSW)
Clinical Director, The Battle Within

———

Jamie is a friend I met through my work with The Battle Within. She is the clinical director of the program and comes from a long career in social work.

Her original plan, she says, was to study business. But in her late teens, she was invited to her state capitol for an advocacy day in support of better mental health programs, and she was intrigued. She decided to focus on an undergraduate degree in psychology before going on to earn her LCSW a little later in life. Jamie says she feels like she's a natural social worker. It's just always been a fit.

Her early years were spent working with women and children in a substance abuse facility. This was her first exposure to the trauma of others. She remembers hearing about the trauma these people endured, and not really knowing how to help, because she lacked the worldview that would have provided the real-life context she needed.

While earning her master's degree and license, Jamie continued to work, first with the children, then the women, at the treatment center. She began to realize the serious mental and emotional injuries caused by trauma, and knew she needed a better understanding because it was clear that these women could never fully heal unless they dealt with the underlying cause of their problems: trauma.

She, along with a colleague, created an eight-week therapeutic trauma awareness program that included sharing stories, breathing, grounding exercises, and other self-care skills and tools as a way to help these women develop self-awareness and coping strategies.

Jamie's next move was to community mental health. Again, she observed that almost everyone coming in was affected by trauma. Also, this is when she became aware of secondary trauma, which is the trauma endured by helpers and caretakers. Secondary trauma occurs when we are exposed to and impacted by the trauma of others. On top of this, she started to realize how many of the helpers came into the profession with trauma of their own.

What she didn't realize then, but openly discusses now, was that she could not fully understand the depth, breadth, and devastation of the trauma that was plaguing the people she was serving because she had not experienced trauma herself. And then, the unthinkable happened.

TURNING POINT

In June of 2017, Jamie's teenage son, Jake, was murdered by one of his friends, and this changed *everything*. As Jamie puts it, "It not only changed everything, it changed who I am."

Prior to experiencing her own trauma, Jamie says she was confident in her ability to deal with stress and the trauma of others. She was good at solving problems, she thrived in crisis mode, and she enjoyed the rush of satisfaction from knowing she was helping people.

In the aftermath of her son's death, she began to view trauma through a new lens. Previously she had understood, anecdotally and clinically, how trauma impacts a person. But now she was living it, and feeling it, and watching what it was doing to the people she loved most. Her understanding of trauma was now visceral.

One thing that became clear to her was that a lot of people who think they are caring for those experiencing trauma are not doing a very good job. When she returned to work, she didn't feel supported by her organization, and she didn't feel their actions toward her were trauma-sensitive at all.

This experience left her with a brand-new awareness and became a turning point for Jamie. It opened her eyes to just how stressful her job had been, and rather than feeling proud that she was able to handle so much, she now knew she needed better self-care.

This realization motivated Jamie to take a deep dive into learning about trauma. She set out to learn what trauma does to the brain and body, and that course of study led her to what she does today. Her entire life is focused on teaching and supporting others in learning more about trauma and doing better. Her hope is that the more we understand about the science of trauma, the better we can help others and ourselves.

She is, in my opinion, a perfect fit as clinical director of The Battle Within. She has lived experiences of severe trauma, has devoted her life in service of others, and possesses the knowledge and empathy needed to work with this traumatized warrior demographic.

TOOLS

These are the tools Jamie has found most helpful on her healing journey:

- Connecting with other trauma survivors and child loss survivors.

- Understanding how trauma affects her brain and body, and knowing what helps her feel better.

- Truly understanding empathy and knowing when she's not operating from a place of empathy.

WHAT NEEDS TO CHANGE

- Leadership culture needs to change. Leaders need to honor the stress, stories, trauma, and secondary trauma of the people doing the work. They need to find a way to allow people to be vulnerable and even fall apart temporarily if that's what they need, because that is part of the healing process.

- Normalize connecting and talking. Connecting and talking does not mean drinking together after work. These people need to connect with each other on a deep level and talk about what they experience.

- Stop waiting until people are twenty or thirty years into their career before introducing wellness and resilience education and support.

Lastly, she asked an important question. "Why can't these teachings and programs be integrated into academy training?" This is a question being asked by many now, and I believe we will begin to see major changes in the way we train our warriors in the not-too-distant future.

CHAPTER 12

Fire/EMS

——

As I'm working on these interview write-ups, I'm finding it amusing to remember how I met some of these great people. Kenny, for example, is a LinkedIn connection. He connected with me after reading my first book, *Mindfulness for Warriors*. Once we were connected, he messaged me, and I'm going to share a little of our early conversation with you.

Kenny: I just read your book, *Mindfulness for Warriors*. Absolutely awesome way to write a book for anyone, but especially for first responders. I had a lot of "me too"s as I read the stories. Thank you for what you do and allowing the stories to be told.

Me: It's so meaningful to hear from people like you who understand, who have done the work. Thank you so much for taking the time to reach out. I'm working on a second book and I'm currently interviewing more people, which is my favorite part. Good people doing good work who deserve our support...deserve to retire healthfully. I'm grateful for your message.

We chatted back and forth after that, and the more I learned about his story, the more I considered him for the book. So, I got brave one day and asked if he would allow me to interview him. Thankfully he said yes, and here we are!

Kenny's journey with the fire service began as a senior project in high school, with volunteer hours at his local fire department and learning CPR. Reflecting back, he says, "When I walked in the door of the firehouse for the first time, it felt like family." He started volunteering at the age of eighteen.

After graduating high school, Kenny went off to college to study mechanical engineering. On his nineteenth birthday, he went to an EMT class, where he met the woman who would become his wife. He graduated from college with a degree in mechanical engineering and went to work for Procter & Gamble, working on deodorant packaging.

He says that job did not feel like a fit. He started to realize he wasn't built to sit inside the same building all day. The work was okay, but it didn't light him up in any important way.

When Kenny and his now wife were on their honeymoon, 9/11 happened, and that tragedy served as Kenny's inspiration and impetus to change careers. Fire service and EMS suddenly felt like a calling. So, he decided to become a paramedic, in spite of a pretty serious fear of needles.

I included that last part because I found it fascinating. Imagine a person who is terrified of needles becoming a paramedic! But Kenny explained he's uncomfortable with needles poking into *his* body. He has no problem with them being injected into other people's bodies. Makes sense.

DIFFICULT EXPERIENCES

Kenny says that, for him, there is not one particular "worst" call that sticks out in his mind. Rather, it was an accumulation of calls over years that wore him down.

He says there are certainly calls that stand out, and the most difficult were always the ones involving children. When he was a brand-new paramedic, he worked on his first fatality car accident. An eighteen-year-old girl had been killed by a drunk driver. He was young, and new on the job, and says that was a very tough experience for him to process.

Another distinct memory is a call that involved a five-year-old little girl. He remembers trying with everything in him to save her, but he couldn't. At the time, his own daughter was five, so this incident hit him extra hard.

I've heard countless similar stories from people who have tended to injured and deceased children that looked like their own children or were about the same age as their own children. This is a chilling experience for first responder parents. But for the most part, like everything else they endure, nobody talks about it in any meaningful way.

Kenny was really shaken after the death of the little girl. He even attended her funeral, which he says gave him some closure, but didn't help to answer all the questions he had about why terrible things happen to innocents. This is a question that haunts many people across these helping professions.

TURNING POINT

Kenny's big turning point came around the time he was eligible to retire. When he hit the twenty-year mark, things were really beginning to pile up. The stress of the job was impacting his personal life. COVID had caused a litany of problems over the previous couple of years, not the least of which was mandatory overtime, which was creating problems at home and in his marriage.

Once he was eligible to retire, his wife encouraged him to do so. He didn't feel like he was finished with the profession yet, but ultimately, he agreed with his wife and made the decision to retire.

Kenny retired from the fire service on September 1, 2022, at the rank of lieutenant.

Even though Kenny had voluntarily retired, he was unhappy. He felt totally cut off from the department and the people who had been like family. He was, of course, removed from department communications and emails, which he expected. What he didn't expect was how hard it would hit him.

He felt lost, and he started using alcohol every day to help him cope, something he had never done before.

Around this time, Kenny was invited to get involved with an organization called Brothers Helping Brothers, a nonprofit that helps and supports firefighters. He decided to go, and he wanted his wife to join him. She was hesitant at first—scared, trepidatious—but she agreed to go. They decided they would go together and attend one day of the event. (Side note: any spouse who has watched their warrior suffer from the devastating and painful impact of a traumatic career in public safety or the military understands this trepidation. I'll discuss this more in the segment for spouses and families.)

Kenny says it felt good to be there, to be around firefighters, and to be involved in something like this. The first day was great! It was filled with good speakers talking about health and wellness in fire service. Kenny and his wife enjoyed it so much they decided to stay for a second day.

There was a guy attending who Kenny knew from peer support. During the event, this guy managed to get Kenny's wife alone and had a private conversation with her. He expressed concern about Kenny, which scared her, so she agreed to swap phone numbers with him, in case she ever needed to reach out.

The next day, the first speaker was a man by the name of Jake Clark, from an organization called Save a Warrior. Jake is in fact the founder of Save a Warrior, and an individual who has done a lot to improve the lives of veterans and first responders.

Kenny remembers Jake being an excellent speaker and says Jake's presentation had a huge impact on him. But at the time, he didn't feel ready to ask for help. He was still holding things in, bottling things up, and he wasn't ready to face those things.

At the end of his talk, Jake announced he had two spots available for the next Save a Warrior cohort, and asked who was ready to go. Kenny was *not* about to raise *his* hand, no way. But, out of the corner of his eye, Kenny saw his friend from peer support put his hand in the air. He said, "I'll go, but I want to take someone with me." Kenny remembers thinking, "*Don't you dare say my name!*" But he did, indeed, say Kenny's name.

Although his friend from peer support did not end up attending the Save a Warrior cohort, Kenny agreed to go, and to this day, he calls that one of the best decisions he's ever made. Save a Warrior is a three-day program for first responders and veterans that Kenny credits with saving his life.

According to Kenny, he left there a changed man. For one thing, the Save a Warrior program requires participants to have been sober for thirty days prior to attending. So, Kenny stopped drinking a month before his cohort, and hasn't had a drink since. He says he replaced drinking with meditation.

Kenny continued to do the work at home and remembers being on a two-week high of feeling great after the program. Then, he hit a road bump and backslid a little. However, he knew he had the option to reach out to the supportive friends he had made at Save a Warrior, and he did. He still does from time to time. He says he is beyond grateful for those connections. They've helped him through some really rough patches post-program.

I want to interject briefly and address the previous paragraph. As I've mentioned in other segments of this book, a theme that arises frequently when I talk to warriors who are on a healing path is that healing is not one-and-done. I don't want to give anyone the impression that if you just start meditating, or go to a couple of therapy sessions, or attend a three-day program, you'll be fine.

No, healing is a process. There won't be any single intervention that magically fixes things for you. It will be a combination of things, practiced regularly, over a period of time, that will help you. And, you'll have to keep it up. You'll need to pay close attention and notice when you start to slide back into old habits or patterns of behavior, and then you'll have to make adjustments. It will be hugely helpful if you have a person or a group of people you can turn to, confide in, and lean on, so that when you hit a rough patch, you won't give up.

TOOLS

Here is a list of tools Kenny has found most useful on his healing journey:

- Support system (he says without them, he would not be here)

- Save a Warrior

- Meditation and mindfulness

- Peer support

- Exercise

- Health and wellness apps

- Therapy

- Yoga

- Pet therapy

- Stellate ganglion block

STELLATE GANGLION BLOCK

Stellate ganglion block—or SGB—is something I've been hearing about for a while but didn't know much about until I talked to Kenny. I have since spoken to others who have had this procedure, and so far, all have reported positive results.

A stellate ganglion block is an injection of anesthetic medication into a collection of nerves at the bottom of the front side of the neck. It's used to treat a host of circulation and pain issues, and it may help mental health conditions and decrease the effects of PTSD.

Kenny had been hearing great things about this procedure, so he pushed through his aforementioned intense fear of needles and got the first injection after attending the Save a Warrior program.

I was surprised to hear that he noticed immediate relief after the first injection. I asked him how immediate the relief was and asked him to give me an example of what the relief felt like.

He said it instantly took the edge off of the inner intensity he had been feeling 24/7 prior to having the shot, and that it caused a noticeable reduction in anxiety. He went on to say that on the way home from the procedure, his wife was driving, and a police car came up behind them with lights on and siren blaring. His wife noted that he hadn't had a reaction to it, and to his astonishment, he became aware that he hadn't reacted at all.

Prior to the SGB, Kenny said, he would have had a big reaction and would have immediately gone into hypervigilant mode. But instead, he felt calm. He was shocked at his lack of response to that stimulus. His predominant feeling was relief.

I learned from Kenny that SGBs are not permanent. They have to be repeated. He also shared that he didn't notice the same level of impact with the second injection, but the third one was the most effective of all.

In between SGB treatments, Kenny continued to work on himself, focus on self-care and wellness, and keep up with therapy.

WHAT NEEDS TO CHANGE

Kenny would like to see wellness and mental health education prioritized at the outset and offered on a regular basis throughout the career, alongside other mandatory training. He says administrative support for this is crucial, and that spouses and families should somehow be included, because the first responder life is hard on them, too.

He'd like to see high-quality, vetted resources readily available to all first responders in every agency and organization. (Especially vetted and culturally competent therapists and clinicians.)

He wonders if health and wellness incentives might help first responders embrace wellness education, and he notes that broad acceptance and support of this type of training will help eliminate the stigma that prevents people from seeking help.

One important thing Kenny pointed out that nobody else mentioned was that organizations should pour resources into recruiting and retention to relieve the pressure to work overtime, which he says is extremely stressful on marriages and home life.

Something he mentioned that others I've spoken to also touched on is gossiping and judging. He says this is prevalent among first responders. Several people I talked to while writing this book discussed how gossiping, judging, and even bullying create a negative and hostile environment, and serve to perpetuate the shame and stigma that cause silent suffering.

CHAPTER 13

ARLO

Corrections | Jail Administrator

I love Arlo's story about why he got into law enforcement. It reminds me of my dear friend, Wendy (host of the *Guns & Yoga* podcast), telling me how watching *Charlie's Angels* inspired her to be a cop.

Arlo told me that, as a kid, he was obsessed with the hit show *CHiPs*, which was a crime drama based on the work of the California Highway Patrol. Watching that show, he says, made him want to get into law enforcement. He's not the only one who loved *CHiPs*. I probably watched every episode, but mostly because I had a crush on Erik Estrada.

When Arlo was twenty-four years old, he became a corrections officer. He originally thought he might want to be on road patrol, but after experiencing that world, as you'll see in the next section, he changed his mind and transitioned to jail administration, where he has dedicated twenty-seven years of his life.

During his career, Arlo brought peer support to his organization, and he serves as Peer Support Commander. For four years he served as Crisis Negotiation Commander. He is very well-trained and well-versed in de-escalation tactics, and he even created a course on *personal* de-escalation, to help people learn how to improve their response to difficult situations. He also brought a program called *Stepping Up* to his institution. Stepping Up is a national initiative developed to reduce overincarceration of people with mental illness.

DIFFICULT EXPERIENCES

As a young corrections officer, Arlo was working his way into a position on road patrol, as I mentioned before. That assignment would have entailed serving warrants, among other duties, and he thought it sounded interesting. One evening, while he was riding along with a night deputy during field training, they went on a call that was reported as a car accident.

When they arrived at the scene, it wasn't a car accident. It was a seventeen-year-old kid who had shot himself in his car, and they determined he had consequently bled to death. That was a bit of a wake-up call for Arlo. He found it disturbing and difficult to process, and it really stuck with him. He began to wonder if road patrol was for him. He ultimately decided he wasn't a fit and turned his attention to jail administration.

Of course, Arlo has witnessed and endured a lot in his twenty-seven years of corrections work, but what he pointed out as an ongoing, difficult issue for him is his inability to turn his feelings off. He refers to himself as a sensitive guy, so much of what he has seen and experienced as a correctional officer has impacted him and stays with him.

Now, I know the word "sensitive" holds a negative connotation for some people, but I've got news for those people. Most of the warriors who confide in me about job-related struggles admit to being sensitive. You know why? Because they are human. No matter your gender or profession, you are a human being, just like the rest of us, and we're all born with the same set of emotions. We are sentient beings, not robots. We have awareness, cognitive abilities, and the capacity to have feelings. Being sensitive is not a weakness, it is your nature.

As I mentioned in Darren's segment, the act of turning off your feelings is called emotional detachment, and it causes people a whole lot of problems.

Having said that, I understand there are times when you have to keep your emotions out of your professional life. I realize that, in certain circumstances, you must shift into professional mode, or warrior mode, in order to do your job, and that might require turning off emotion. I believe this comes easier to some people than others. The problem is that some people lose the ability to turn their emotions back on when it's safe and appropriate to do so, and this negatively impacts their personal lives.

TURNING POINT

Arlo describes his turning point as slow. Rather than one isolated event, he recounts an accumulation of circumstances over many years that led him to seeking and accepting help and support.

A primary marker in time was a few years ago, when he attended a full day of training presented by a mental health professional who was a military veteran. She had been diagnosed with PTSD and talked openly about it. Arlo says he learned a lot from that training, and he related to much of what was discussed.

During that presentation, the instructor recommended a program for first responders and veterans. This was a program she had attended, and as an alumna, she highly recommended it.

Arlo decided to look into the program she recommended, which is offered by an organization called The Battle Within. He ultimately applied and attended. He has since returned to the program as a mentor.

As I've already mentioned, The Battle Within provides a free five-day retreat in nature designed for veterans, first responders, and frontline medical personnel. The curriculum was created by a combat veteran who is now a therapist. I have provided the meditation and mindfulness instruction for this organization since 2018, and that's where I met Arlo. (You'll find more information about The Battle Within in the resource section of this book.)

Arlo says those five days changed his life. Prior to attending, he remembers his anxiety was at an all-time high. He recalls feeling hopeless and in a very dark place.

After The Battle Within, Arlo says he felt like a different person. He felt a little raw for a while, and says he found himself crying easily, which is something he had previously held in. He also remembers feeling anger rising up quite a bit, but instead of repressing it, he allowed himself to process it. He used the skills he had learned at The Battle Within to process the emotions as they arose.

He went on to say that he felt like he had been sort of torn down and built back up. He admitted to experiencing a lot of ups and downs after the program, but he rode the waves by applying the tools he had gained and working through things.

Arlo explains that this work helped him open up and allow himself to be vulnerable. He has had to apply patience, but overall, he's much better because now he has tools. This has opened up a world of possibilities for him in terms of wellness, self-care, processing emotions, and continuing to heal.

TOOLS

These are Arlo's favorite wellness tools:

- Breathing

- Meditation

Arlo is an open-minded guy. He says he was always open to the concept of meditation and would use it here and there over the years, but he never really got focused on using it to help improve his mental health and overall well-being until he attended The Battle Within.

As I mentioned, that's where Arlo and I met. After his cohort, he reached out to me, and I'm going to share part of what he had to say:

"Kim—Thank you for spending a cold, blustery, snowy day with us [at The Battle Within]. This program truly changed my life... I wish your husband would've had a resource like TBW... Not gonna lie, your story was painful to hear, but you are changing hearts and minds. You are awesome and I thank you from the bottom of my heart."

Isn't that the kindest message? Arlo and I have kept in touch since then, and I consider him a friend. I even got to meet his wife at a workshop a few months ago. I feel fortunate that I get to meet so many amazing people in this line of work.

WHAT NEEDS TO CHANGE

This might be my very favorite answer of all. It is short and to the point and gets right to the heart of things.

In answer to this question, Arlo quickly and simply said, "We need to get rid of all the macho bullshit. Leaders and administrators need to get on board with health and wellness and commanders need to model it."

Well said, my friend.

CHAPTER 14

Law Enforcement

———

Erik is a member of the Pause First Academy team of trainers, and a friend. We met in January of 2018, when I held a meditation and mindfulness train-the-trainer class for twenty-one first responders and retirees. During the interview for this book, he and I chatted and reminisced a little about that training.

He told me my class was the first and only place he had ever seen someone teaching meditation to first responders specifically, so as a retired police officer, he was really interested. He also said my training helped him on his path, which I obviously appreciated hearing. He said he found it eye-opening and inspirational, and listed it as one of his turning points.

At that same training, Erik also met Angela Caruso-Yahne. Since then, Angela, too, has become a Pause First Academy trainer. She's an EMS Chief, a military veteran, a mindfulness instructor, and a certified chaplain. (I meet the coolest people in this line of work, and I'm beyond grateful!)

I interviewed Angela for my first book, *Mindfulness for Warriors.*

Erik introduced Angela to a local organization called Midwest Alliance for Mindfulness, for which she is now an instructor. Angela familiarized Erik with the Upaya Institute Chaplaincy Program, and he went on to enroll in and complete that program and is getting ready to embark on his first journey as a chaplain with a local police department.

In college, Erik studied music. He's a musician at heart, and still plays and performs at local venues. One of Erik's jobs after college was mall security. There, he met and got to know several police officers, and he became interested in their work. They encouraged him to apply with the police department, so he did.

Back then, Erik says, it was hard to get into his local police department. It was very competitive, and they would typically hire one person per several hundred applicants. He didn't make it through the first time, but he was determined, so he joined the National Guard and got trained as a military police officer. Then he went back to the police department, and this time he made it through. Erik served in law enforcement with the same agency for twenty-five years.

Because Erik is a friend, I'm probably going to go on a little bit about him and his background, primarily because, to me, he is a mystery wrapped in an enigma, in the best possible way.

When you meet Erik, you get a grounded vibe. He's calm, intelligent, and well-spoken. He comes across as introspective, kind, and mild.

So you can imagine my surprise when I met a retired police officer who, when he found out I knew Erik, said, "I worked with Erik. Great guy. He's a badass!"

I said, "Are we talking about the same person? Erik, the daily meditator? The teacher of mindfulness teachers? The musician?"

The guy went on to say, "Yeah, he's a good dude. He was an excellent police officer and leader, but he's also quite the badass. He's a defense tactics guy, was an instructor, and is very skilled in Krav Maga."

"Skilled in what?" I asked.

"Krav Maga," he said. "You know, Israeli street fighting? Israeli defensive tactics?"

"Um, no, but I will be Googling it immediately."

And I did. Hoo boy, yeah. That Krav Maga (Krahv Mah-GAH) is no joke.

When we met for this interview, I asked Erik all about this. I was determined to peel back his layers. What other secrets might he be hiding? Is he Batman?

He's not, but I did learn that while he was a police officer, he became very interested in self-defense and defensive tactics. So, on his own, he traveled to Los Angeles to become a certified Krav Maga instructor. Then, he and another officer pitched Krav Maga to their department, and the department adopted it as their defensive tactics program.

Erik wore a lot of hats during his time in law enforcement. He was a street cop for about a year before getting recruited to deep undercover narcotics. This proved to be extremely challenging when he started having children. He felt like he was living a double life—two totally different identities. The strain became untenable, so he started to consider other options.

One day at work, he noticed an ad on a bulletin board, seeking an SRO (School Resource Officer). SROs were brand-new to his area at the time, and he was intrigued. He applied and got it. He started by splitting his time between a middle school and a high school, ending up as a full-time SRO at the high school.

Erik was an SRO for about three and a half years, and he says it was one of his favorite assignments of all. He describes his time as a school resource officer as being a teacher, a counselor, and a cop. He had his own office at the school, and he delivered seventy to eighty presentations to the kids each year.

Prior to his installation as a full-time SRO, Erik says the kids at this high school, who came from predominantly low-income homes, were often subjected to harsh treatment by the adults in their lives—

parents, school officials, and the police, which was the opposite of what they needed.

One way Erik supported these kids as their SRO was by teaching them the legal consequences of their actions and behaviors. He wanted them to know their rights, be informed, and get a fair shake. One of his favorite presentations focused on the Fourth Amendment to the Constitution, and the students' Fourth Amendment rights.

The Fourth Amendment protects people from unreasonable searches and seizures by the government, but there are a lot of exceptions. He taught the students about consent and that they had the right to say no to a search if the officer did not have a warrant.

Erik tells the story of a fellow officer who found out about this and lost his mind. He thought it was wrong to be teaching the kids this stuff, and he made a big deal out of it. This caused a bit of a confrontation between the two officers. Luckily, Erik had a friend in the department—a grizzled old veteran cop—who caught wind of this and stepped in. He said to the angry officer, "Why wouldn't you want these kids to know their legal rights? You're a parent, you have kids. You don't think these kids deserve to know their rights?" Thankfully, that shut the argument down, and Erik continued informing and educating his students about the law.

One very heavy memory Erik carries with him from his days as an SRO happened over a weekend. On a Friday night, Erik took his toddler daughter to his high school's football game. While they were there, a fight involving some of his students erupted. He helped to break up the fight and sent everyone on their way. He thought that was the end of it.

Unfortunately, later that weekend, one of his students, who had been involved in the Friday night fight, murdered someone. Erik was devastated. To this day, he remembers every detail about that kid. He could tell me his full name, when he was convicted, what his sentence was—everything. He laments that he really struggled with some of what happened in his years as an SRO, and still does.

Looking back, Erik wishes he had done that job longer, but at the time he wanted to promote to detective.

Next in Erik's career, he applied to be a detective. He got it and spent the next seven or so years on investigation assignments. Over his long tenure, Erik worked in Residential and Commercial Burglary, Criminal Intelligence, TAC (Tactical Team), and Professional Standards. He says he disliked Professional Standards so much that he quit policing and was gone for about ten months but ended up going back.

He remembers always saying that he never wanted to promote. He just wanted to do the job. But he was recruited to continue promoting, and motivated by the pressure, he ended up promoting to sergeant, then lieutenant, and then captain within just a few years. As a leader, Erik worked midnights for eight years, and he says that was the beginning of the end for him. As Operations Commander on the midnight shift, he felt isolated, and the overnights were taking a toll on his nervous system, his physical and mental health, his marriage, and his home life. But he felt trapped.

Things got so bad that he started applying for jobs outside of law enforcement, and this was twenty years into his career. His financial advisor told him that in terms of his financial future, he needed to stay twenty-five years, so he did.

DIFFICULT EXPERIENCES

The first thing in Erik's career that caused him indescribable pain, trauma, and stress was not work-related. In 1991, just about one year into Erik's career, his younger brother died by suicide.

When Erik returned from bereavement leave, a lieutenant approached him with his leave request, angry that Erik hadn't filled it out properly. The lieutenant offered no condolences and no compassion, just a searing reprimand for failing to fill out a form correctly.

Also during this time, a fellow officer made an off-the-cuff and callous remark about suicide victims, which caused a verbal altercation between Erik and the officer. They ended up having a conversation and the officer apologized. But not long after that, in a separate incident, a sergeant made a flippant comment about a person who had taken their own life. Erik remembers the comment being cruel, insinuating that the person had no value because he had killed himself.

To make matters worse, within a very short period of time after Erik's return to work, he had three separate encounters with suicide calls. Those were extremely difficult for him to process, physically and practically, but also mentally and emotionally.

All in all, this was a very rough time. Not only did Erik lose his little brother, but he didn't feel like the people in his organization handled it very well.

A side note about this traumatic and devastating time in Erik's life: he felt then, and still believes to this day, that the investigation of his brother's death was handled poorly. He says as a brother, but also as a cop with a lot of experience investigating crimes, that the investigation was insufficient. He believes there was evidence that his brother might not have died by suicide, which made it even more difficult to accept, and prolonged the grieving process.

One unusually difficult case that stays with Erik was one involving a young girl who was abducted from a local department store and was reported missing. They had found the girl's car in a different parking lot, but they couldn't find her. Erik was the sergeant on duty. He had received a lot of missing persons calls in his career, but when he got this one, he knew in his gut it was a serious case, and that foul play was probably involved. The girl's body was found a few days later.

At the time, Erik had a daughter who was the exact same age as the girl, and even shared the same name. As many other first responders have reported, this made the case extra difficult and overwhelmingly emotional.

Other than these heartbreaking examples, Erik says there's not really any one case or single thing he can point to that caused him the most harm. Rather, he points to an accumulation of stressors, traumas, and organizational stress that weighed him down. And he admits he didn't fully realize the heaviness of this weight until he retired.

There's one last thing that bears mentioning. Erik, like many of the people I speak with across these professions, admits to considering suicide at times. He says it got worse after retirement, when he no longer had the distraction of the job and was forced to face the fallout. He says this was not solely due to the job but involved layers and levels and an entire lifetime of things that piled up over years.

TURNING POINT

Erik calls his first turning point a *subtle* one. During the time he was a sergeant, he attended a seminar presented by Dr. Kevin Gilmartin, author of *Emotional Survival for Law Enforcement*. He says he learned some important things there, but he viewed the presentation through the lens of, *how do I take what I learned here and become a better sergeant?* He didn't apply the knowledge he gained to his own experience, which is why he refers to it as a subtle turning point.

Unspoken subtext: *I'm fine, but I want to do a good job and take good care of my people.*

I know that last part probably inspired an "Uh-huh, that sounds familiar" from a lot of you, whether you've thought it, or observed it from your leaders. This is common, even prevalent. I see it all the time: Well-meaning leaders who want the best for their folks and bring in leading-edge wellness training, but don't take advantage of it themselves.

Erik's true turning point was retirement. Retiring forced him to face his emotions, not run from them or bury them, which is what he admits he had unconsciously done throughout his career. When he started to face his emotions, he realized he was not okay. Facing his feelings led him to therapy, which he says made a *big* difference for him.

From his very first therapy session, Erik says he jumped right into telling his therapist everything, without holding back, and this felt liberating. He remembers feeling physically better, and even being able to breathe better.

Along with therapy, and around the same time, Erik discovered meditation and mindfulness, which became transformational tools for him. He says these practices were easy to embrace, and he feels that is due in part to his many years of discipline with practicing music.

As I said earlier, Erik also listed my meditation and mindfulness train-the-trainer as one of his turning points. When he attended my training, he was already an MBSR (mindfulness-based stress reduction) teacher. My class helped expand his vision of how meditation and mindfulness can be applied and inspired him to think about how these practices could be used to improve first responder performance and well-being.

This leads us to the full array of tools Erik listed as being the most impactful for him.

TOOLS

- Studying and understanding neuroscience

- Studying and understanding trauma

- Meditation and mindfulness

- Therapy

- Integrating contemplative practices into his spiritual life

- A deep, daily formal and informal practice of mindfulness

- Being a part of a local mindfulness community in the form of practicing in groups, teaching, and participating in retreats

WHAT NEEDS TO CHANGE

Erik framed his suggestions around law enforcement because that is his background, but his advice is adaptable and relevant to all warriors.

He believes police officers should be trained in skills that would allow them to cultivate their humanity over the course of their career, to build their capacity for wise decision-making under stress, to open their hearts and minds to their own biases, and to ground the police culture in compassion in ways that demonstrate the effects on the health and well-being of police officers without compromising the safety of the officer or the public.

He offers the following formula:

Traditional contemplative wisdom + modern neuroscience >> mindfulness.

Erik concluded by opining that, over the course of a law enforcement career, occupational stress and trauma has a tremendously negative impact. He says things like empathic distress result in burnout for many law enforcement professionals. He believes training focused on emotional intelligence, cultivating humanity, and restoring resilience can transform police leadership and police culture, and might even contribute to healing the broken relationship between police and our communities.

 DAVID

Law Enforcement | Marine Veteran

—

David and his wife, Danielle, are the founders of an organization called Saint Michael's Warriors. The couple started their nonprofit to help first responders, veterans, active-duty military, and their families through difficult times. They are committed to assisting those struggling with PTS(D), substance abuse, and mental health challenges find and access a pathway to health.

I set out to interview them as a couple, but after hearing their stories, I asked Danielle if she would agree to a one-on-one interview. Thankfully, she said yes, because this story is so multifaceted that I wanted to present it to you from multiple perspectives.

First, there is the perspective of David, a police officer who was shot in the line of duty. Next is Danielle's perspective as David's wife. And then, there's Danielle's point of view as a twenty-year NYPD veteran who spent a good portion of her career in FID (Force Investigation Division) investigating police-involved shootings, among other things.

I'll start with David's story. You'll learn how his line-of-duty injury impacted him, and you'll find out how he was able to recover and heal from that trauma. Danielle will add to this narrative with some of her thoughts and experiences in a separate interview. You'll hear about Danielle's own career and her unique perspective as both a cop and a spouse in the next section.

DIFFICULT EXPERIENCES

Right out of high school, David joined the United States Marine Corps, where he served in active duty for four years. After the military, David got on with a police department, where he served for twenty-two years.

At the beginning of his law enforcement career, when he was about halfway through the police academy, 9/11 happened. That led to him being placed on inactive reserve, and then a little later, active reserve duty. When the Iraq war was declared, David learned from his recruiter that his Marine unit had been "first boots on the ground," and he was torn between staying in law enforcement and going back to military service.

For years, David grappled with guilt over not being there to support his unit during the war, until finally, five years into his law enforcement career, he decided to re-enlist, and he initiated the process to do so. He says his fiancée at the time initially agreed with his decision, but after he started the process, she changed her mind, telling him if he re-enlisted, they were done. So, David decided to continue working as a police officer. He says he sometimes still finds himself feeling guilty over not returning to military service.

A few years into his law enforcement career, David responded to a call about a house fire and a possible female trapped in the house. He was the first on scene, and when he arrived, the woman's son was outside of the house, screaming that his mom was inside.

David grabbed his fire extinguisher and made his way into the house. He tried to get to a closed bedroom door where he could hear the woman screaming, and what he heard still haunts him. "Help me, I'm burning, I'm on fire!" The woman screamed these words over and over. He tried with everything in him to get to her, but he was completely overcome by smoke and couldn't proceed. Not long after this, a backup officer arrived, and the two of them made several attempts to reach the woman, to no avail.

When the fire department arrived, they were able to pull the woman from the house, but she succumbed to her injuries on the way to the hospital.

After this incident, David was consumed by guilt and the memory of hearing the woman's screams for help. He says he was not in good shape, and he couldn't sleep. Looking back, he says there was nowhere for him to turn, no help available for him to process that incident.

David's father was a firefighter who had been widely hailed as a hero for rescuing a family from a burning house, so David went to him to talk about this. He asked, "How did you do that? How did you save those people? And why were you able to do it, but I wasn't?" His father's reply was, "Son, I'm a firefighter. I've been trained and I had gear and a mask. You're a cop. You didn't have any of that." Even though his dad gave him this gift of exoneration, David could not shake the guilt. And he says, to this day, he can hear the woman's screams.

The final and most difficult experience in David's career happened in 2020. There was a man who was wanted for attempted homicide in another jurisdiction, but he lived in David's jurisdiction. They had credible information that the man was in possession of an AK-47 and had mental health issues.

David was called on to assist with this case, and after some cat-and-mouse investigation by him and other officers, he determined there was no good way to approach the suspect's apartment without being seen, so he knew they would have to do a vehicle takedown to get the suspect in custody.

He parked outside the suspect's residence, at the end of an alley, where he could see the suspect's truck. The police had received calls from the suspect's neighbors saying that he had been seen loading guns and ammunition into his truck and appeared to be getting ready to leave.

David remembers having a bad feeling, so he called his wife to let her know what was happening. He made a couple of other calls while he waited, and then he saw that the suspect's truck was on the move. He immediately called his chief and got permission to call in SWAT and the state police for assistance, and made sure a search warrant was being prepared.

He was undetected by the suspect at first, as he was following at a distance and a normal speed. There were two state troopers behind him. Pretty quickly, he realized the suspect had become aware that he was being followed, and a brief car chase ensued. All of a sudden, the suspect stopped his truck in the middle of an intersection, diagonally, in a tactical position. Then he jumped out of the truck holding an AK-47 and began firing at David's car.

David started to engage the suspect through the windshield of his patrol car, but, realizing he was pinned down and under heavy gunfire, he made the decision to exit the car. He advanced toward the suspect on foot, still exchanging gunfire. He did his best to flank the suspect while continuing his advance. By now the two state troopers had exited their vehicles and were firing as well. The suspect was hit in the hip and the foot, fell to the ground, and surrendered.

During the shootout, David's police car was hit ten times. He suffered a gunshot wound to his arm, torn ligaments in his knee, permanent hearing loss in his left ear, and a potential TBI (traumatic brain injury). He was also later diagnosed with PTSD (post-traumatic stress disorder).

TURNING POINT

This incident was definitely the beginning of a turning point for David, but it wasn't immediate. He tried outpatient treatment for several months and worked with two different therapists, but he says he kept getting worse.

By this point, he was in such bad shape that his wife insisted on inpatient treatment. She says his alcohol use and post-traumatic stress symptoms were off the charts, and she knew he needed serious help. David agreed to inpatient treatment, stopped drinking three days before entering, and hasn't had a drink since. This was his big turning point.

After completing the thirty-day program, David says he kept up with intensive outpatient care for a few months. He also flew to Kansas City to attend The Battle Within's five-day retreat. In fact, that's where he and I met. We had a brief chat in which he told me that he had read my book, *Mindfulness for Warriors*, and that he had learned about The Battle Within from the book.

Flash forward to just a few months ago, when David reached out to let me know he and his wife were starting a nonprofit organization. After speaking with him a little more extensively and hearing his story, I asked him if he would be willing to speak with me for this book. Also in that conversation, he reminded me that he had learned about The Battle Within from my first book. I asked him how he found the book and he said he got it from his wife, who had learned about it from a psychologist.

He said his wife, Danielle, came home one day, handed him the book, told him to read it, and added that she had already highlighted a bunch of passages. So, this is how Danielle got pulled into an interview for this book. I, of course, wanted to talk to her as well, and when I found out she was a twenty-year veteran of NYPD, I was really intrigued. I was so happy when she, too, agreed to an interview.

Before moving on to my last couple of questions, I asked David how he stays on track with healing and well-being. He told me that he has continued with therapy, and he attends a weekly support group for first responders. He also attends weekly AA meetings to maintain his sobriety.

TOOLS

Here are the tools David has found most helpful on his healing journey:

- Yoga—He's a huge proponent of yoga and practices regularly.

- Therapy—Private sessions and group therapy.

- Telling his story—He finds that telling his story is therapeutic and healing.

- Meditation

- Breathing—His favorite breathing exercise is box breathing.

Something David pointed out, that I think is important to mention, is that tools he uses now did not work for him in the beginning—for example, box breathing. So, if you're new to healing or you haven't quite gotten started yet, please keep that in mind. You might not be ready for tools like breathing or meditation at the onset of your healing journey. Your nervous system might simply not allow it at first. But don't toss out any tools you learn. Keep them in your back pocket, because they could very well become necessary daily habits in the future.

WHAT NEEDS TO CHANGE

David wants to see legislation that supports mental health expenses being covered by worker's comp. He believes mental health should be treated the same as physical health.

He also thinks agencies need to up their game on mental health training. Instead of an occasional boring video that just checks a box, he supports regular mental health check-ups with zero penalty. He says these check-ups should happen frequently, so support can be rendered at the onset of problems instead of waiting until there is a crisis.

And lastly, he wants to see the stigma around mental health kicked to the curb. I could not agree more. Organizations need to put an end to any judgment around mental health issues and get focused on the well-being of their employees.

CHAPTER 16

DANIELLE

Law Enforcement

———

As you already read in David's story, I met Danielle as a result of setting up an interview with her husband. But after learning more about this couple, I knew they had an important story to tell, together and separately.

Right out of high school, Danielle went to college to major in criminal justice. She says she took the police test when she was eighteen or nineteen, but she had to be twenty-one before they would hire her. Exactly one day after her twenty-first birthday, 9/11 happened. She had already started the hiring process, but everything was put on hold for a while. Then, in November of 2001, she got a call from NYPD, and entered the police academy in July of 2002. Her academy class was the first post-9/11 class.

Danielle spent about eighteen months on foot post, then worked patrol for a few years. She later worked in narcotics, organized crime, and FID (Force Investigation Division).

She also married a cop. I've always thought it would be really hard to be a law enforcement couple. It seems like the stress, long hours, overtime, and everything else that comes with the job would be difficult to navigate. But then again, I guess nobody understands all of this better than another cop.

I really enjoyed talking to Danielle and learning more about her life and career. She's a true warrior. She even played competitive soccer until she was forty! Who does that?! It's so impressive!

Danielle is a retired cop, a mother to two sons, a positive force with a great mindset, and a true partner to her husband. But it wasn't always easy, as you can imagine. In fact, after her husband's shooting, things got so bad that she basically had to give him an ultimatum to get him into treatment.

DIFFICULT EXPERIENCES

Danielle says her husband's shooting and the fallout afterwards was hands-down the most difficult experience of her life. But before we get into that, let's take a look at a few of her work-related experiences.

When I asked her about job-related stress and trauma, she said she had always done pretty well handling the stress of the job, until she got into FID investigations. She says that's when the job really started to take a toll. She was a detective investigating police-involved shootings, use of force, police homicides, and officer suicides.

She touched on a couple of shootings she investigated that really got to her. The first one she mentioned happened while an officer was in pursuit of a domestic violence suspect and the suspect shot him in the head and killed him.

The second one involved two officers sitting in a THV (temporary headquarters vehicle). A guy climbed up on the side of the vehicle and shot one of the officers in the head through the window. The officer's partner called 911 screaming, "My partner's been shot! My partner's been shot!"

Now, remember, Danielle was an investigator. So, when these incidents happened, she had to work the cases, listen to the 911 calls, watch body-worn camera footage, process the crime scenes, and voucher evidence. As we learned from Brenda in my first book, it's heartbreaking, devastating, and traumatizing on a whole different level when it's one of your own—someone who wears the same uniform you do.

Danielle says toward the end of her career she could no longer stand to watch the body-worn camera footage. There was one really terrible incident involving an officer shooting one of his own, and just a few months before she retired, two officers were shot while responding to a domestic violence call. She had stopped watching the camera footage, she just couldn't do it anymore, and that's when she knew it was time to retire.

HER HUSBAND'S SHOOTING

The shooting was David's trauma, but the impact on Danielle was crushing. Never underestimate the pain and suffering caused by secondary trauma—being exposed to and impacted by the trauma of others.

After David's shooting, and once police had the suspect in custody, another officer noticed David was bleeding. He asked David, "Are you okay? Did you get hit?" David brushed him off, "Naw, I'm fine. Probably just got cut up from the glass in my car." And what happened next is shocking.

They took him back to the police station.

David had just been in a full-blown shootout and was bleeding, and they took him back to the police station instead of taking him to the hospital.

And then his wife arrived.

Upon arrival, Danielle went into warrior mode. She immediately pulled the bandage off of her husband's arm, said, "You've been shot." Then, she insisted he be taken to the emergency room, immediately. At the ER, doctors determined he had indeed been shot, and they went about pulling bullet fragments from his wound. According to David and Danielle, this was just one of many mistakes that took place after this incident.

This is where Danielle's worlds collided. She had spent a good amount of time on the investigation side of line-of-duty shootings during her years with the Force Investigation Division, but she had never experienced the officer perspective, or the spouse point of view. Being on the other side of the investigation was an eye-opener for her and, on top of all of the other stress, trauma, and fallout she had to endure, she was also grappling with the collision of these multiple perspectives.

After the shooting, things got really bad for the couple. David was of course traumatized, but he didn't have the awareness or tools in place to process the trauma, so he turned to alcohol. This is, as you know, the most common coping mechanism among warriors. But the fact is, it doesn't really help anyone cope. It just temporarily numbs a little of the pain, and then makes *everything* a whole lot worse.

Reflecting back, Danielle says David had always used alcohol to mask anxiety, which she says was there long before the shooting happened, but absolutely exploded after this incident. She says his drinking, mood, and demeanor became unbearable, and she insisted on an inpatient program to help him get sober and deal with his mental and emotional health.

"It was basically an ultimatum," she says.

David agreed to go and signed himself into a thirty-day inpatient program. Danielle says this was one of the most difficult things either of them had ever faced. But more importantly, it turned out to be one of the steps that saved his life and saved their marriage. She's proud to report that he's been sober for over two years now.

TOOLS

Here are the self-care tools Danielle finds most useful:

- Reading
- Breathing
- Stays away from alcohol
- Healthy diet
- Exercise
- Doesn't watch news
- Limits social media

Lastly, she shares a quote from a psychologist that she thinks is one to live by: "Lessen your exposure to trauma." Now, this might seem like an obvious suggestion, but how many warriors spend time chasing the adrenaline rush and engaging in behaviors and activities that keep them exposed to stress and trap them in a trauma loop? There are a lot of choices you can make to help regulate your system and offset the effects of trauma. Limiting social media and news might be a good starting point.

WHAT NEEDS TO CHANGE

I found it so interesting that Danielle answered this question by first saying that she really felt like mental health services were readily available in her agency, NYPD. It's refreshing to hear from someone that they felt like their organization had sufficient services and support in place. I almost never hear this, but I believe we'll start hearing it more and more.

She followed this by saying, "But I know in most agencies, the services and support need to be more easily accessible."

Danielle believes that regular mental health check-ups are a must and should be conducted every few months. She also feels these organizations should add regular classes and small group discussions to address the inevitable mental health issues of the job.

PART III

THE OTHER WARRIORS

CHAPTER 17

SPOUSES AND FAMILIES

—

So far, we've focused primarily on the warrior perspective. But now, I'd like to bring spouses and families into the conversation. Behind every warrior, there are family members who navigate their own unique challenges. There's a crucial aspect of this warrior narrative that often goes unnoticed and underserved—the families of first responders, veterans, and other warriors; their spouses and children. In this chapter, I'll discuss some of the unique struggles and challenges they face and explore ways we can support these forgotten heroes.

These families are the unsung heroes at home, offering unwavering support while living with the constant uncertainty and stress that come with having a loved one in a warrior profession. In most households, if Mom or Dad goes to work in the morning, or leaves for a business trip, nobody worries about them being traumatized, getting injured, or never returning home. But in a warrior household, that is a very real concern, and a concern usually kept to oneself.

LIVING WITH A WARRIOR

In 2018, I wrote an article that was published in *American Military University/In Public Safety* online and *Police1 by Lexipol* online. In it, for the first time publicly, I opened up about some of my husband's struggles and how they negatively impacted our life together.

It was a hard thing to do, and I was terrified to publish it, and for good reason. One of my husband's family members was very upset with me and even refused to speak to me for a while, feeling I had unnecessarily aired my husband's dirty laundry. But here's the thing. Sometimes these warriors take their frustrations out on the people closest to them. And for way too long, warrior families were expected to just take it and stay quiet about it.

There are many reasons why family members haven't been able to speak up about their own stress, trauma, and suffering. In law enforcement, there is a constant threat hanging over everyone's head that if the warrior or anyone in the family gets into any trouble at all, the warrior might lose their job.

It is true that law enforcement professionals are held to high legal standards, but there have been times when this threat cloud of dismissal has loomed so dark and heavy over law enforcement households that domestic violence, alcoholism, drug abuse, threats of suicide, and other issues have gone unreported. The warrior is afraid of what their organization might do, and the families are afraid of what the organization or the warrior might do, so everyone stays quiet and lives with the pain and the shame.

Now, this won't pertain to everyone, but I have spoken to a lot of veterans and first responders over the years who have admitted being unstable, inconsistent, hot-tempered, withdrawn, militant, angry, depressed, and volatile at home, and just not very good partners or parents. I've spoken with a whole lot more who have admitted to alcoholism.

Oftentimes, the spouse who is not in a warrior profession becomes codependent or complicit in this behavior, just doing their best to navigate it themselves and keep the family going. But what's almost always true in these situations is that nobody in the household is equipped to manage what is really going on, which is typically underlying stress, trauma, unresolved childhood trauma, and mental and emotional issues that, if addressed and treated, can be healed, and overcome.

I am going to include my full article here in this chapter. It's written from a law enforcement perspective, and I use words like *officer*. But please, don't get hung up on that. Whether you are a cop, a firefighter, a social worker, a probation officer, or in any of the other many, many professions that fall under the warrior umbrella, please take the message that is intended. As I said in my introduction, trauma did not get the memo delineating professions.

What I know to be true is that many of you are suffering, but don't know what to do or who you can safely turn to in order to get help for your spouse, your children, yourself, or the entire family. There are others of you who want out of your marriage, but you are afraid. Everyone's situation is different, but one thing many of us have in common is shame. As you'll read in this article, I shared some things about my life with David that I hadn't shared with even my closest friends because I loved my husband and I wanted to protect him, but also, if I'm honest, I was embarrassed about just how much shit I put up with.

NOTE TO SPOUSES

My hope is that sharing this article will help someone feel less alone. I heard from a lot of people after the article was published who shared similar experiences and feelings, even if their spouse was still living. The article talks about my husband's inability to show vulnerability because of his profession, it touches on the trauma he carried, and it peels back the curtain on some of what I experienced as a result of his unresolved trauma.

This article highlights a shooting, which was a pivotal and traumatic event in my husband's life. But, as we know, it's never any one thing. Along with the haunting memories of the shooting incident, David carried years of unresolved trauma from a thirty-year career in law enforcement, and honestly, from traumatic incidents across his entire lifetime. Maybe you will recognize something in my story that will relate to issues with your spouse.

NOTE TO WARRIORS

I am not sharing this article or bringing up these difficult subjects to beat up on you. If you are wrestling with inner demons and that is hurting you and hurting your family, I hope something in this book helps you let your walls down, set your pride and fear aside, and take some small step toward healing. As you've learned from the warriors in this book, it is never too late. This might be the single most important step you ever take in your life.

Disclaimer/Trigger Warning:

This article addresses my husband's suicide and may be too difficult for some of you to read. Please proceed with caution.

MY HUSBAND'S SUICIDE: RECOGNIZING PREDICTORS OF POLICE SUICIDE

In order to survive and thrive in the law enforcement culture, my husband felt he could not afford to be vulnerable.

Last year, more law enforcement officers died from suicide than in the line of duty. Sadly, suicide rates are thought to be much higher than reported—it's widely accepted that police suicide is woefully under-reported, especially when counting those—like my husband—who commit suicide after retiring.

My husband, David Colegrove, was a law enforcement officer for thirty years. He killed himself in 2014, less than three months after he retired. Since his suicide, I've learned a lot about trauma, post-traumatic stress, secondary trauma, hypervigilance, and the common predictors of suicide among law enforcement professionals and other first responders.

First and foremost, I've realized that my husband and I were sitting smack dab in the middle of all of that, and we didn't even know it. David carried a tremendous amount of trauma that had roots in his early years, grew exponentially throughout his police career and affected all areas of his life.

THE IMPACTS OF TRAUMA

Trauma happens when someone experiences or witnesses abuse, victimization, neglect, loss, violence, and disasters. Unfortunately, the majority of first responders experience some kind of trauma during their career and it can be toxic to them mentally and emotionally.

In my husband's first year of policing, when he was only twenty-one years old, he was involved in a shooting, and someone died. He was called into the police station, where his badge and gun were taken away and he was sent home. For days he did not know what was going to happen. Then he got a call telling him he had been cleared and should report to roll call the next day. And that was that. Back to work. No counseling, no conversation, and no support of any kind.

In the years that followed, the untreated and unprocessed trauma caused David to experience reoccurring stress symptoms, which he was intermittently able to numb—typically with alcohol. Over time, accumulated stress and trauma grew so overwhelming and so powerful that it infiltrated his personality, turning an otherwise great guy into an angry, paranoid, cynical character, or an emotional wreck who could not stop crying.

These stress-induced symptoms ultimately left my husband unable to cope with change, uncertainty, or the most basic daily challenges.

THE DARK SIDE OF THE LIGHT OF MY LIFE

It has taken me a long time to summon the courage to speak honestly about my husband, his issues, and our struggles. David was a very proud and private man, so telling his secrets feels like a betrayal of sorts.

I don't want to let strangers into the dark corners of our life together. I'd much rather talk about the good times, and there were plenty of those. Anyone who knew us knew that we loved each other deeply and shared an intimate friendship that I may never know again. But when I think about keeping the truth to myself and ignoring all the bad things, I think about those officers who are living with such pain today, right now, and I know I have to tell the truth in hopes that they may avoid the same fate as my husband.

The truth is, there was a dark side to David that cast a shadow on our otherwise sunny life—like a murky figure lurking in the background. When David got emotionally triggered by anger or felt threatened in any way, this dark figure would step out of the shadows and take over. This happened rarely, but when it did, it was intense.

That dark guy was never violent toward me, but he was angry and hateful and completely out of control. After each "episode" had subsided, David was embarrassed, ashamed, and apologetic. And even though these episodes were awful, I felt so sorry for my husband because it was clear he was full of pain. I believe this dark alter ego developed as a result of years of unresolved trauma and suffering.

THE VULNERABILITY PARADOX

I observed and endured a lot of dysfunction as a result of my husband's unresolved trauma. This is extremely difficult for me to admit because I feel vulnerable exposing the underbelly of my imperfect private life. I guess I'm afraid of being judged.

As I identify this feeling of vulnerability within myself, I realize this is the very fear that gripped my husband and kept him from seeking the help he needed. I have deep compassion for this man who, in order to survive and thrive in the law enforcement culture, felt he could not afford to be vulnerable.

That's the tangled web, isn't it? Officers are hurting or are scared, but they want people to think they're okay. Everyone else seems to be doing just fine. If officers are honest about their struggles, if they say they need help, others may think they are weak or broken or crazy. Not to mention the fact that officers could face demotion or dismissal from their job. So, they stay quiet. And they suffer.

The deeper I get into my work with first responders, the more I realize how important it is for me to let my guard down and speak the truth about my husband's problems and our mostly awesome, but sometimes awful, life together. There are too many people suffering in silence and *way* too many people dying. I hope that David's story—

our story—will shine a light on this reality so others won't have to endure the same pain and tragedy.

THE UNRAVELING

In the year leading up to my husband's death, his mental health became increasingly worse. His decision to retire after thirty years triggered a surge of anxiety, and although he had spent two years carefully crafting a new business venture with a partner, David was terrified of the uncertainty of civilian life and wallowed in thoughts about worst-case scenarios.

In hindsight, there were all kinds of warning signs during that year. David's anxiety intensified and the "episodes," which were almost always alcohol-induced, became more frequent. The dark guy surfaced more often and brought with him fear, worry, angst, paranoia, and irrational behavior.

David's last day at work was Friday, September 5, 2014. On Saturday we had his retirement party. On Sunday he had a full-blown anxiety attack, and by the following week his anxiety sent him to the emergency room. This kicked off two months of intense inpatient and outpatient treatment and the slew of prescription medications did not help. In fact, they made things worse.

He barely made it through Thanksgiving dinner because the anxiety was so intense that he could not sit still, or focus, or even carry on a normal conversation. Two days later, David drove to the back of our neighborhood, sat in his truck, and shot himself.

COMMONALITIES AMONG POLICE SUICIDE VICTIMS

If you or someone you know is experiencing the following symptoms, especially if multiple symptoms are concurrent or repetitive, please seek help immediately:

- Chronic stress
- Depression
- Anxiety
- Anger
- Intense irritability
- Aggression
- Alcohol abuse/alcoholism
- Drug use/addiction
- Hopelessness
- Isolation/withdrawal
- Suicide ideation
- Talk of suicide

Don't hesitate. Don't wait. Don't let your pride get in the way. Reach out to someone and tell them you need help, then accept the help, and do whatever it takes to feel better and live better. Know that what you're experiencing today is treatable, you can recover from this, you can feel better, and you can go on to live your best life. I only wish that I had the knowledge I have today about the impacts of trauma and the treatment options available to have gotten the help for David that he needed and deserved.

AN AFTERWORD TO THE ARTICLE

In the years since I wrote that article, I've heard from and talked to many people who suffered for far too long because pride, shame, embarrassment, fear, anger, rage, helplessness, and hopelessness kept them from seeking help. Some didn't take a step toward healing until they encountered a tragedy or were otherwise forced to. *You can make a different choice.*

As I write this, warriors around the world, who are struggling with untreated mental and emotional issues and often substance abuse, are unconsciously and unintentionally sabotaging their relationships and hurting their children. Spouses are feeling overwhelmed and helpless to intervene. Neither partner in the marriage knows where to go or what to do for support and relief, and the children are caught in the middle of the chaos.

There are many more support and treatment options specifically for veterans and first responders now than there were a decade ago when our family lost David. We tried to get help for him at the time, but we didn't know about warrior-specific programs, which I believe might have made a difference for him. The traditional psychiatric track we put him on didn't help him, but that doesn't mean it won't help you.

One of my greatest frustrations around my husband's death was how resistant he was to the kind of help that could have made a difference for him. He felt embarrassed and weak because of his mental health issues, and he refused to go to the hospital to detox when I became alarmed about how the prescribed psychiatric drugs were affecting him. I knew he was taking a dangerous, although prescribed, combination of medications, and I could see the medications were not having their intended effects on him.

On top of all of that, he never stopped drinking alcohol, which I believe also contributed to the rapid and total decompensation of his mental health, which ultimately led him to make the decision to end his life. I know now that it was the only way he could see to end the suffering. I also know that was never true.

Whether you are the warrior, the spouse, a parent, or a sibling, if what you're reading in this book sounds familiar, it is time to make a move in the direction of support, help, and healing. I'm not saying that every warrior in emotional distress is going to take their own life, but I am saying that ignoring emotional distress always ends badly, in one way or another. Plus, I hate to think of you waiting one more day to take a difficult but meaningful step that can open doors to a new and better way of living for everyone involved.

HELP FOR WARRIOR FAMILIES

Here are just a few ideas of ways that organizations and communities can offer support for family members:

1. Mental Health Services for Families:

    Provide ubiquitous access to mental health services for spouses and children of veterans and first responders. These services should be readily available and affordable and should address the unique stressors they face.

2. Education and Resilience Training:

    Offer workshops and training programs for families to help them understand and cope with the challenges of their experiences. Building resilience and coping skills can empower families to navigate the uncertainties more effectively and can set kids up with coping skills that will help them the rest of their lives.

3. Peer Support Groups:

Establish peer support groups for spouses and children to connect with others who share their experiences. These groups can provide a safe space for sharing, healing, and seeking guidance.

4. Family-Friendly Policies:

Encourage organizations to implement family-friendly policies that allow warriors to be active and engaged members of their own families. No parent should have to routinely expect to miss holidays, birthdays, practices, games, performances, school events, and family gatherings while their children are growing up.

5. Outreach and Community Engagement:

Promote community engagement and awareness about the challenges faced by warrior families. Encourage community events and activities to provide support and resources to these families.

7. Breaking the Stigma:

Foster a culture that destigmatizes seeking help for mental health challenges in warrior families. Normalize conversations about mental health and well-being, and help these families emerge from the silent suffering that has ruled their existence for too many generations.

I've worked with a few organizations that focus on support of families, but I'd like to see a lot more of this. Just as a warrior's mental and emotional health are part of their overall health, so too are their relationships a part of their holistic well-being. The entire family must be considered as we improve our support of warriors.

In the next chapter I'll introduce you to Rachel and Jeremy. They offer a great example of how important it is to include family members in this conversation, and they provide a beacon of hope for couples and families who are struggling alongside their warrior.

CHAPTER 18

RACHEL & JEREMY

Rachel, Licensed Professional Counselor
Jeremy, Fire Service

I knew I wanted to include spouses and family in this book. In fact, it's been suggested that I write an entire book for the family members of first responders and veterans, and it's something I am considering.

In my first book, *Mindfulness for Warriors*, I wrote about my husband's dark side, and how it impacted our marriage, which was a very hard thing to do. What I suspected then, and I know now, is that relationship issues are prevalent in the first responder and veteran world, but it's a bit of a dark secret.

There are many reasons for this, and while we can't place 100 percent of the blame on the job, the fallout from the job contributes mightily. I've learned that addiction, infidelity, and domestic abuse are not uncommon, but what is common, is the shame and secrecy that accompany these issues.

When I opened up and pushed myself to be vulnerable and tell the truth in my book, I knew that my discomfort was nothing compared to the relief it might bring a person who was living a similar story and hiding it from the world.

As we know, a high percentage of marriages end in divorce. In the US, the number is estimated at around 40–50 percent. For first responders, that estimate shoots up to 60–75 percent, and the divorce rate for combat veterans is closer to 80 percent.

With that in mind, I am bringing you an important story of one couple's darkest days, and their journey back to each other. I'm going to introduce you to Rachel and Jeremy. Jeremy has been a firefighter for almost two decades, and Rachel is a therapist. They were gracious enough to sit down with me and openly share their story, which I believe will not only resonate with some of you but might offer guidance and hope.

JEREMY

First, I'll introduce you to Jeremy. He is a fire captain and has been in the fire service for nineteen years. After college, he worked as a financial analyst for three years, then switched to fire service when he realized he was not cut out to sit in an office.

RACHEL

Rachel is a therapist with a background in ministerial services. Her undergraduate degree was in theology, and after college she did youth ministry and funeral ministry, as well as homebound and hospital services. In grad school, Rachel studied psychology, earning her master of science degree in counseling psychology, and she has worked as a licensed professional counselor since 2014.

She says she has always been service-driven. As far back as she can remember, she felt called to help people, and to be of service to others.

LIVING SEPARATE LIVES

Rachel and Jeremy were married in 2015. Jeremy was already a firefighter, and although Rachel had family in law enforcement and had worked professionally with some veterans and first responders, she notes that she did not have the personal insight and level of understanding of fire culture that you gain as a spouse.

Looking back, she recalls noticing Jeremy's low moods. She says he often seemed depressed and unhappy. She started to realize that he was using alcohol to cope with job stress. As Rachel recounted this part of their history, she began hedging her comments a bit, like she was treading lightly into this topic, and then Jeremy jumped in.

He interrupted Rachel by saying, "I was an asshole. I was a drunk asshole, and I didn't treat her very well. Plain and simple."

Rachel did not disagree with Jeremy's self-assessment, I got the picture, and we moved on. (I will say, it was refreshing to hear someone take full-throated responsibility for their actions in such a forceful way.)

2019 was a rough year for this couple, to say the least. Rachel's father was struggling with Parkinson's and was in and out of the hospital. She and her sister spent a lot of time caring for their dad, and in the middle of this, her sister, who was pregnant at the time, began having serious pregnancy complications. She ended up having an emergency c-section and landed in the ICU shortly after the birth of her child.

That's a lot. But that was just Rachel's side of the family. Around the same time, Jeremy's dad had a stroke, and just one month later, he had a second stroke, which took his life. He never left the hospital after the initial stroke.

When he passed, the couple traveled to Jeremy's home state for his funeral. They agree, looking back, that Jeremy's drinking was really bad while they were there. Jeremy says he knows it was because he was "back home," in his old stomping grounds, plus he was dealing with the stress of losing his father.

During all of this, Jeremy says he was drinking a lot and drinking often. He admits to pushing Rachel away back in those days, and they agree they were basically living separate lives.

CRISIS

One night, later that year, while Jeremy was at the fire station, Rachel had a dream about him being unfaithful. In the dream, a voice said to her, "Trust your gut."

Not long after she had this dream, Rachel received a text from a guy who wanted her to know that his wife and Jeremy were having an affair. She was, of course, shocked and angry. She could not believe that her dream was becoming her reality.

Right away, Rachel confronted Jeremy about the affair. She says he tried to deny it at first, but she wasn't buying the denial, and as they talked, he became extremely emotional. She says he started to emotionally unravel, slowly at first, and then went into full-blown decompensation.

Decompensation is a clinical term for a significant, often rapid, deterioration in mental health. It can present as a progressive loss of normal psychiatric functioning, which is what was happening to Jeremy.

What occurred next quickly escalated everything. In the middle of this confrontation, Jeremy walked away and headed down the hall. Rachel was going to leave the house, but when she got to the door, she heard the sound of a gun being racked. She ran down the hall and found Jeremy in their bedroom with a gun to his head. She says she tackled him and managed to get the gun away from him, and as she was trying to secure the gun, Jeremy went and got a second one.

Fortunately, Rachel was able to get a hold of the situation, and once she did, she called one of Jeremy's firefighter friends, who came over immediately and secured both guns.

Rachel recalls Jeremy being totally dissociated at this point. The friend stayed with him while Rachel left the house to make phone calls and try to get help for her husband.

She was able to get Jeremy into an inpatient treatment program, and this led to a major turning point for Jeremy, and for their marriage. As a result of that program, Jeremy says his perspective completely shifted and he started taking responsibility for things. When he completed the program, he was in a much better place, but not quite there yet. He knew he had a little more work to do.

He started going to regular therapy appointments. He says his first experience with therapy was not a good one. It wasn't the right fit and didn't work out. But he didn't give up. He sought out a different therapist and this one used neurofeedback therapy, which he feels made all the difference in the world for him.

Neurofeedback therapy is a noninvasive treatment that encourages the brain to develop healthier patterns of activity. It aims to change the way the brain responds to certain stimuli. Jeremy credits neurofeedback therapy as an integral part of his recovery and healing.

DIFFICULT TIMES

JEREMY

Jeremy knows now, post-treatment and therapy, that he carried childhood trauma into a job that was destined to pile on more trauma. He knows he mismanaged things for a lot of years and that he always used alcohol as a coping mechanism. But, he says, nothing can prepare you for what you're going to see on the job, and he also realizes now just how unprepared he was.

On his very first day out in the field, Jeremy ran his first suicide. The call led them to an elderly woman and the first thing he noticed about her was that she looked like his grandmother. The woman had been on suicide watch, and therefore everything she could have used had been removed from her room. But she was found in her bathtub, where she had drowned herself.

Jeremy was the one who pulled her out of the tub and administered CPR. Then he had to continue CPR in the ambulance until they got to the hospital, even though he knew she was gone. For multiple reasons, this was an intensely traumatic first call, and one that stuck with him.

He remembers his first child-involved call clearly. A father had fallen asleep on his couch, leaving an infant and a small child unattended.

Evidently, the baby was hungry, and Dad wasn't waking up, so the toddler tried to feed the baby by putting dry formula into the baby's mouth, which basically formed a blockage in the baby's throat. When help arrived, they attempted to save the baby, but they didn't have the full and accurate story, so they were unsuccessful.

What stuck with Jeremy the most was thinking that if they'd just had the details about what had happened, they might have been able to save the baby, and that was a very hard thing to accept.

I don't know if there's anything that can be done to fully prepare first responders and veterans for what they will see, hear, feel, and endure on the job. But I do know we have to do a better job of trying to prepare them. And we need to do a much better job of helping them when the inevitable happens.

RACHEL

Rachel is a therapist, so she spends a good portion of her life listening to the problems, pain, and suffering of other people. She's not a first responder, but she's a helper, and that can take its own toll on a person's well-being.

Obviously, some of Rachel's most difficult times happened in 2019. In that one year, she endured more than most of us will experience in a decade or longer. She admits that afterwards, it took a little while for her to do what she needed to do to take care of herself.

Several months after the incident with Jeremy, he casually mentioned going to a gun range with one of his friends, and Rachel found herself immediately flooded with emotions and images. She became totally overwhelmed—her heart was racing, her breathing was labored, she felt like the world was closing in on her, and she was unable to speak.

I'm going to pause here and recommend a book I read a few years ago. You'll find it listed in the resource section of this book, as it is one I refer people to quite often. The book is by Bessel van der Kolk, and it's called *The Body Keeps the Score*.

What Rachel experienced after hearing her husband talk about shooting a gun was a trauma response. In van der Kolk's book, he explains that trauma gets trapped and locked into our bodies, and when a traumatic memory is triggered, we will sometimes experience very real physical symptoms.

After living through a severely traumatic event in which her husband came very close to shooting himself, Rachel's body instantly recalled all of the trauma reactions she experienced during the incident. You see, the human brain cannot discern between an actual traumatic event and the memory of one. She heard her husband talking about shooting a gun, and her system reacted with same level of intensity it had during the incident months before.

Rachel began to realize she was exhausted. She was struggling to get through sessions with her clients and knew she was burning out. Burnout is common across all helping professions, and oftentimes the helpers neglect their own need for help and support.

At this point, Rachel knew she needed to focus on herself, so she made a conscious decision to cut back on her work schedule. She immediately contacted a therapist and started attending regular therapy sessions. She found EMDR therapy to be profoundly helpful on her healing path and says continuing with therapy is a crucial part of her self-care.

THE GIFT OF CRISIS

According to Jeremy, this life crisis was a gift in many ways. He says recovery and healing are the hardest things he's ever done in his life, but this experience gave him a chance to live a whole life, a real life, as he puts it. He says after treatment and therapy, everything got better. His friendships, relationships, and work life improved immensely. He's much healthier now, and he even looks better!

After the treatment program, Jeremy never drank again, and that undoubtedly contributed hugely to all of his other successes. Also important were his dedication to a healing path, his life, and his marriage.

Jeremy's breakdown and rebuilding helped the couple connect on a deep human level, which allowed them to heal their relationship. They both agree it was the worst thing and the best thing that ever happened to them as a couple. They say everything was shattered, and because they were both willing, they were able to rebuild.

Now, they communicate about meaningful things, not just the trivialities of life. Jeremy says he talks to his wife and shares with her, unlike before. Rachel says if she sees old habits creeping up, she addresses them, and they talk about what's going on.

They are intentional with one another. When they're together, they're careful to be *present*.

Previously, Jeremy admits, he would not listen to any feedback. He says he had a strong need to be right and any feedback at all sounded like criticism. But now, Rachel can provide feedback about their relationship or her feelings, and he is willing to listen. In fact, they both offer feedback to each other, because there is a safety in their relationship that wasn't there before.

TOOLS THEY FIND HELPFUL

Tools Jeremy finds helpful:

- Therapy

- Neurofeedback

- Working on his Jeep

- Camping and off-road trips

- He started a podcast (*The Washdown*) and *this* he says is his most important tool: *talking about things*

Tools Rachel found helpful:

- Her support system: friends, family, and coworkers

- Horses, dogs, and nature

- Exercise

- Therapy

- Stellate ganglion block

- Journaling and writing

- Solitude, peace and quiet

- EMDR therapy

WHAT NEEDS TO CHANGE

JEREMY

- The acceptance that it's okay to go get help. It should not be judged like it is now.

- Organizations need to know about all the programs and resources that are available, and the resources need to be readily available.

- We need more first-responder-specific programs.

- Organizations need to invest in their people up front and often, and they need to stop waiting until someone breaks to do something, like they do with equipment.

I also asked Jeremy, as a Fire Captain, what he sees as the top stressors. He listed organizational stress, staffing issues, and lack of mental health resources and programs.

RACHEL

- These professions need to get out of the *respond to crisis* mode and shift to *prevention* when it comes to their members.

- We must talk about PTS (post-traumatic stress) as injury, not a disorder. These are mental, emotional, and moral injuries, and should be treated the same as physical injuries.

- Everyone needs to be more open and honest about their relationships. She says this can help reduce the shame and stigma associated with mental health concerns and treatment. "We aren't alone," she says.

Based on my work in this area for almost a decade, I couldn't agree more with Rachel's last point. That's why this couple's contribution to my book is so important. People are suffering and relationships are dying, in part, because of the silence. I am the first one to admit that "airing your dirty laundry" is not fun. But what if we reframe it?

What if, instead of associating secrecy, shame, and failure with our relationship problems, we focused on the idea of relationship honesty, maintenance, prevention, and healing? Rachel and Jeremy told us that they can talk and share about meaningful things now because there is a safety in their marriage that wasn't there before the crisis and subsequent healing. So, what if we started a conversation around *creating safety* in first responder and veteran relationships, and we normalized it?

Let's peel back the curtain a little before we wrap up this segment.

It's time for some introspection. Take a nice deep breath and consider how this couple's story made you feel. The feelings that arose when you read their story are important indicators. Are you shocked that they were so open and vulnerable? Are you or have you experienced something similar? If so, does anyone know? And how does your situation make you feel? Were you inspired to take a step? Did you feel hopeful that healing might be possible? Or are you trapped in a cycle of shame, anger, or denial?

There's no right or wrong answer. I'm just encouraging you to take a moment and reflect. Awareness is sometimes the first step toward change.

In general, I view the silent suffering of couples much the way I view the silent suffering of individuals. Seeking help is not always easy, nor is doing the work to fix things. Stigma, pride, mental health issues, stress, and pressure can all get in the way, and change is hard. But if you can find a way to create that safety in the relationship that Rachel and Jeremy talked about, you might be able to break things down and build them back up in a healthier, more loving way.

Usually, it's at least worth a try.

CHAPTER 19

RETIREES

Retirees are near and dear to my heart, for obvious reasons. I lost my husband less than three months after he retired. We had big plans, individually and as a couple. I was working on growing my business, he was preparing to roll out his new business, and we were shopping for RVs. It was a very exciting time, except for his ever-increasing bouts of intense anxiety, depression, insomnia, and nightmares.

Last year, three members of my team and I created a full day of training specifically for retirees and those who plan to retire in the next five years or so, as I explained in Keith's segment of this book. The three of them, Brenda, Wendy, and Darren, are all retired first responders themselves, and Wendy is married to a retired first responder.

All too often, people tell themselves a fairy tale about retirement. They say that's when they'll slow down, enjoy life, and be happy. Spoiler alert: if you haven't faced, dealt with, and processed the emotional baggage you accumulated over the course of your career, a fairy-tale retirement is not very likely.

Where do you think all of that stress, pain, grief, anger, and trauma you've been stuffing down goes? Are you hoping it will evaporate on the day you retire? I don't mean to be overly direct or negative, but that's not going to happen. If you are still employed, and planning to retire in the next few years, I encourage you to engage in serious introspection, and to make some kind of plan to prepare yourself mentally and emotionally.

Based on my own experience and the many, many stories I've heard over the years, I implore you to take some time to consider the commonly unexpected emotional and mental challenges of life beyond the job.

The word *retirement* often conjures images of leisurely days, newfound freedom, and a relaxed pace of life. But for first responders, military veterans, and others, the transition to retirement can be a complex journey, and one that can catch you off guard. As warriors step away from roles that have defined their identities for years, they often find themselves grappling with thoughts and feelings they never expected.

In my case, after my husband was officially retired, he had to return to his office to pick up retirement credentials. When he left our house, he seemed fine. When he got back home, he seemed agitated. The first thing he said to me was, "It's like I never existed. They already have someone in my office." I was honestly surprised that he was surprised, but I felt compassion for him. He had been in the same line of work for thirty years, and just like that, it was over.

Never in a million years could David have predicted he would feel that way. In his mind, he was ready to go, and ready to move on. He was completely unaware of just how deeply he had identified with his career. He didn't take the time to emotionally disentangle or release himself, because he didn't know he needed to. Overidentifying with the job is common across warrior professions.

HOLDING IN EMOTIONS

This, more than anything, causes warriors problems after retirement. First responders and veterans often develop a coping mechanism that involves suppressing their emotions throughout their careers. The demands of the job require them to stay focused, composed, and resilient in the face of adversity. Holding their feelings at bay so they can perform their duties effectively is imperative. But they become adept at compartmentalizing, ignoring, and turning off their feelings.

However, emotional suppression can come at a cost. It can lead to a disconnect from emotions and a lack of practice in processing them. Retirement can abruptly strip away the distractions and responsibilities of the career, leaving the individual to confront a surge of emotions they may not be equipped to handle.

COMMON EMOTIONAL AND MENTAL CHALLENGES AFTER RETIREMENT

1. Depression: Many retirees experience feelings of sadness, hopelessness, and a sense of purposelessness. The loss of identity and structure can contribute to these emotions.

2. Substance Abuse: In some cases, individuals turn to substances like alcohol or drugs to cope with the emotional upheaval of retirement. This can lead to addiction and further complicate their mental and emotional health.

3. Nightmares: Retirement can trigger vivid nightmares and flashbacks related to past traumas or unresolved emotions, making sleep disturbances a common issue.

4. Post-Traumatic Stress Symptoms (PTSS): Retirees may experience post-traumatic stress symptoms, including intrusive thoughts, flashbacks, and heightened anxiety. These symptoms can be related to their service or to unresolved emotional issues.

5. Post-Traumatic Stress Disorder (PTSD): For some, retirement can exacerbate or bring to the forefront underlying PTSD, which requires a diagnosis, and may have been suppressed during their career.

PREPARING FOR THE MENTAL AND EMOTIONAL ASPECTS OF RETIREMENT

While retirement can be emotionally challenging, mental and emotional problems are not an inevitability.

Here are some steps that first responders and veterans can take to better prepare for the emotional and mental aspects of retirement:

1. Mental Health Check-Ups: Regularly consult with mental health professionals, well before retirement. Establishing this routine can help identify and address underlying issues before they become overwhelming.

2. Explore New Interests: Before retirement, start exploring new interests, hobbies, or passions that can provide a sense of purpose and fulfillment in your post-service life.

3. Build a Support System: Cultivate a strong support system of friends, family, and fellow retirees who understand the challenges you're facing. Lean on them for emotional support and guidance.

4. Emotional Intelligence Training: Consider emotional intelligence training to reconnect with and understand your emotions. This can help you process them more effectively.

5. Physical Health: Prioritize physical health through regular exercise, a balanced diet, and adequate sleep. Physical well-being is closely tied to emotional and mental health.

6. Therapy and Counseling: Don't hesitate to engage in regular and consistent therapy or counseling when needed. Professional guidance can provide you with strategies to manage emotions and mental health effectively.

7. Meditation and Mindfulness: Practice mindfulness and meditation techniques to increase your self-awareness, to become more attuned to your emotions, and to manage stress and anxiety.

8. Stay Engaged: Find ways to stay engaged with your community, perhaps through volunteering or mentorship programs. Staying connected can foster a sense of purpose.

It's becoming more common for organizations to reach out to their retirees. Some agencies include them in peer support, and others have outreach channels to help retirees transition and stay connected. However, this area needs a lot of improvement.

More often than not, warriors feel isolated, left out, and lost when they initially leave the job. It's typical for retirement to hit people harder than they imagined, and we unfortunately lose a lot of warriors within the first few years of retirement—some to suicide, others to health issues often exacerbated by lifestyle choices.

It would be great to see organizations help create a separation strategy for their folks in which people getting close to retirement would have training and support to help them prepare for the aspects of retirement they might not be considering. Then, creating ways for retirees to stay connected and engaged, *if they want to,* would be ideal.

PART IV

DEBRIEF & RESOURCES

CHAPTER 20

KEY TERMS

—

In this section, I'm going to provide definitions and explanations for some of the key terms that describe common mental and emotional issues that impact warriors during and after their careers. I want to emphasize the word *common*, because I know how many people feel alone, broken, or weak, when they find themselves struggling with mental and emotional problems. But you're not any of those things.

These problems are prevalent. However, traditionally, nobody wanted to admit to them. So, everyone just kept going along acting like everything was okay. Thankfully, we are beginning to put those days behind us and get honest about the real and legitimate fallout of being a warrior, protector, guardian, or healer.

ADVERSE CHILDHOOD EXPERIENCES (ACES)

Let's start here. This is something a surprising number of warriors endured long before they entered their profession, and a phenomenon that many people are unaware of.

Adverse childhood experiences, commonly known as ACEs, refer to a range of traumatic events or adverse situations that individuals may have faced while growing up. These experiences can include household dysfunction (like substance abuse or domestic violence), physical or emotional abuse, neglect, and other difficult and harmful circumstances.

ACEs have gained significant attention in recent years because of their profound and long-lasting impact on physical and mental health. When it comes to veterans and first responders, childhood trauma can manifest in various ways. Warriors may struggle to manage the high-stress environments they work in, leading to burnout and intense emotional strain.

You can learn more about ACEs on the CDC's website. Go to www.cdc.gov and search "ACEs." There's also a simple ten-question test you can take to get an ACE score and find out how much childhood trauma might be affecting your adult life.

STRESS

When we're stressed, our brain releases hormones into our system like adrenaline and cortisol. This sets off a chain reaction of physical responses that can include increased heart rate, muscle tension, and even digestive problems. Warriors often deal with stress overload. On the job, you've regularly faced high-pressure situations that triggered your body's stress response (the fight-or-flight response). That repetitive state of alertness can lead to all sorts of mental and emotional health concerns, like anxiety, depression, and even post-traumatic stress disorder (PTSD). But that stress doesn't clock out when you do. It can follow you home, and even follow you into retirement.

CHRONIC STRESS

Chronic stress is a long-term state of emotional and psychological strain caused by challenges, pressures, and demands. Unlike short-lived stressors that give you a temporary adrenaline rush, chronic stress is persistent, and it wears down your biological systems. It's the kind of stress that can impact every aspect of your life, affecting your mental, emotional, and physical health, your relationships, and the overall quality of your life.

TRAUMA

Trauma is like a deep, invisible emotional wound that hasn't healed. It's caused by profoundly distressing and disturbing experiences. It can disrupt relationships, work, and day-to-day functioning, and may lead to mental health conditions like depression and anxiety. Left untreated, trauma can cast a long shadow over your entire life, causing insomnia, flashbacks, nightmares, hypervigilance, and other mental, emotional, and physical symptoms.

SECONDARY TRAUMA

Secondary trauma occurs when individuals are exposed to and affected by the trauma of others. If you think about it, this pretty much describes life as a warrior. Warriors regularly witness distressing and traumatic situations, and these experiences take a toll. Symptoms of secondary trauma can mirror those of post-traumatic stress disorder (PTSD).

VICARIOUS TRAUMA

Vicarious trauma is widespread across all helping professions. It occurs when individuals are repeatedly exposed to the traumatic experiences of others, leading to their own emotional and psychological distress. Signs and symptoms of vicarious trauma can include emotional numbness, intrusive thoughts, increased anxiety, and a heightened sense of vulnerability. Perhaps one of the most significant aspects of vicarious trauma is how it can reshape a person's worldview. It can make them more attuned to the darker aspects of human existence, challenging their beliefs and trust in the world's inherent goodness.

POST-TRAUMATIC STRESS

Post-traumatic stress is a mental health condition that occurs in individuals who have experienced or witnessed a traumatic incident. This condition can lead to chronic stress, disrupted sleep, depression, severe anxiety, and strained relationships. It can also lead to hypervigilance, where individuals are constantly on edge, or avoidance behaviors, where they'll do anything to avoid reminders of the trauma.[2]

---

2 You can suffer from symptoms of post-traumatic stress without having been diagnosed with post-traumatic stress disorder (PTSD).

POST-TRAUMATIC STRESS DISORDER

Post-traumatic stress disorder, or PTSD, is a clinical diagnosis. It is a psychiatric disorder that occurs in people who have experienced or witnessed a traumatic event, series of events, or set of circumstances.

Those diagnosed with PTSD may have flashbacks, nightmares, severe anxiety, and emotional numbness, often interfering with their daily life and functioning.[3]

MORAL INJURY

Moral injury occurs when a person feels they have betrayed their conscience, moral compass, values, or beliefs by taking part in, witnessing, or failing to prevent an act that violates their personal principles. It can cause overwhelming and persistent feelings of guilt, shame, and remorse. Moral injury is pervasive among veterans, first responders, and healthcare professionals.

COMPASSION FATIGUE

Compassion fatigue is a state of emotional, physical, and psychological weariness or exhaustion that results from continuous exposure to the pain, trauma, and suffering of others. First responders, healthcare workers, and pretty much everyone who works in a helping profession is at risk of experiencing compassion fatigue. Signs and symptoms

---

3 It's important to note that many individuals suffer from post-traumatic stress symptoms without meeting the *diagnostic criteria* for PTSD. This is often referred to as *post-traumatic stress symptoms,* or PTSS.

may include feelings of emotional numbness, apathy, reduced feelings of empathy, and a general lack of sensitivity. I've heard it described as, "My give-a-shit meter is stuck at zero."

BURNOUT

Burnout seems to be an epidemic across all service-oriented and helping professions. It's a state of physical, emotional, and mental fatigue resulting from chronic workplace overextension. Burnout is particularly prevalent in professions where high-pressure situations, overtime, and heavy workloads are the norm. Signs and symptoms may include feelings of cynicism, persistent exhaustion, decreased productivity, and a growing sense of ineffectiveness.

EMOTIONAL DETACHMENT

Emotional detachment occurs when we knowingly or unknowingly turn off our connection to our emotions. It's a muting or a numbing of our feelings. While it can serve as a form of protection, it can also lead to an inability to feel joy or happiness, difficulty maintaining healthy close personal relationships, and a diminished desire or ability to be loving and affectionate with our family.

HYPERVIGILANCE

Hypervigilance is extreme or excessive vigilance. It's a state in which an individual experiences heightened levels of anxiety, alertness, and anticipation of danger.

HYPER-INDEPENDENCE

Hyper-independence is a stress response that causes people to feel they must make decisions and accomplish things without the support of others. Some signs of hyper-independence are difficulty trusting others, delegating to others, and forming close or long-term relationships with others.

HYPER-RESPONSIBILITY

Hyper-responsibility, also known as an inflated sense of responsibility or hyper-responsibility syndrome, is a belief or a cognitive bias by which a person feels they are personally responsible for people and events outside of their control.

POST-TRAUMATIC GROWTH

Did you even know this was a thing?! Well, it is, and it's something I'd love for you to consider and maybe even aspire to.

Post-traumatic growth is a theory that supports the idea of personal growth after a crisis or significant life challenges. It involves a positive psychological transformation that occurs in the aftermath of trauma.

Sounds too good to be true? Or maybe even impossible?

Think of it as a beacon of resilience that can emerge from the depths of adversity. For warriors who regularly face high-stress and traumatic situations, post-traumatic growth can be a coping mechanism as well as a personal growth tool. Instead of being solely defined by the negative impact of traumatic experiences, individuals may experience personal growth, gaining new insights, and finding a greater appreciation for life.

The saying "Grow through what you go through" is an encouragement to view hardship as an opportunity for personal development and transformation. The experiences of a warrior can be extremely difficult, but you can develop the ability to identify and extract insight, lessons, and wisdom from the experiences, and integrate these takeaways into your future to increase resilience and well-being.

STRATEGIES FOR NURTURING POST-TRAUMATIC GROWTH

- Fostering Resilience: Building emotional resilience through education, training, and self-awareness can help individuals better cope with stressors.

- Peer Support: Participating in open dialogue and peer support within the profession can provide a safe space for sharing experiences and promoting growth.

- Mental Health Resources: Engaging with mental health resources and counseling can help individuals process traumatic events and develop strategies for growth.

- Mindfulness and Self-Care: Practicing mindfulness and self-care techniques can promote emotional healing and personal growth.

- Training and Education: Ongoing learning in the areas of stress management, wellness, self-care, work-life balance, and coping skills can empower individuals to navigate the challenges of their profession more effectively, increase resilience, and foster personal growth and development.

CHAPTER 21

PEERSOURCES

*The trusted modalities, tools, and support
mechanisms recommended by your peers*

———

I made up a word for this section. *Peersources* are resources that your peers have found useful and would recommend to others. I've compiled a complete list of every tool mentioned by your fellow warriors in this book. I hope you'll find it helpful as you plan and strategize your personal healing journey.

Before we jump to that list, I want to share a final interview.

Justin Hoover is a friend and the director of The Battle Within, one of the resources I most often recommend to people. He's been involved in the warrior wellness space for a long time, and as someone who sits at the helm of an organization dedicated to helping veterans, first responders, and frontline healthcare workers heal, Justin has keen insight into this aspect of the warrior world. I thought he'd be the perfect person to include in this section of the book, since we're talking peersources. He *is* one, and he runs one.

JUSTIN

Executive Director, The Battle Within
United States Army Veteran

Some of you will remember Justin from my first book, *Mindfulness for Warriors*, or the reboot version, *The Mindfulness for Warriors Handbook*. Justin and I met several years ago when I reached out to him about the possibility of being an instructor for his organization. Thankfully, a few months later, he brought me into the fold. Teaching meditation to warriors at The Battle Within cohorts is one of my very favorite things.

When we jumped on the phone, Justin was trying to make his way to his office. He made a comment about missing a turn on his way, and then dropped in a quick off-the-cuff comment about his TBI (traumatic brain injury). That led into a conversation we didn't intend, but looking back, this is where the conversation needed to go.

At first, I thought he was making a joke. He *kind of* was, but in truth, he was just acknowledging something he's had to learn to live with.

BRAIN INJURY

When Justin was a young infantryman in Iraq, he survived twenty-two IEDs (improvised explosive devices) and two car bombings. He was injured in the second car bombing and was awarded a Purple Heart. The TBI was not diagnosed until much later.

He doesn't actually know how many TBIs he may have suffered, and he doesn't know exactly how the brain injury has impacted him overall, but he does know he was fundamentally different after the head injury.

During The Battle Within cohorts, attendees complete a personality test to help them better understand themselves. The test they use is based on the work of Jungian analysts Robert Moore and Douglas Gillette, and separates individual personalities into four types: king, warrior, magician, and lover.

Justin says prior to the brain injury, he was definitely a warrior type, as it relates to the aforementioned personality test. He says he was an action-oriented, decisive problem-solver. So, when he took the test, he expected to match with the warrior archetype. But it turned out he was more closely aligned with the magician.

This realization led to some important introspection. Justin realized that, unlike his pre-car-bomb self, he needed a little more time to process information. Rather than being someone who would decisively jump right into any situation with full life force, he had become a person who needed a moment to digest information, reflect, and make a more thoughtful, measured decision.

Also, before the head injuries, he considered himself a visual learner. Now, he says, he is a kinesthetic learner.

Prior to stepping onto a healing path, Justin says these changes were challenges. He was trying to be the way he was before, the way he had always been. The healing journey taught him to accept the transformation, work toward understanding it, and learn to live in acceptance of who and how he is now.

We need to know so much more about TBIs and their long-term and wide-ranging effects. I shudder to think how many people are walking around with undiagnosed brain injuries. And I get a heavy heart when I think about the ones who *have* a diagnosis, but no support to navigate the challenges.

THE REVENANT JOURNEY

This conversation between Justin and me segued into a theme that has emerged in the writing of this book: Healing is not a one-and-done proposition, it is a journey.

The Battle Within, for example, is a five-day group therapy program, created by fellow warriors, to help others suffering from PTS(D) understand the traumas they have endured while operating in service of others. TBW provides an introduction to integrative tools that set the stage for healing. They call the program *The Revenant Journey.*

Justin posited that it can be difficult to convince some people to take that first step onto a healing path, because often what they're looking for is a quick fix. Depending on their degree of struggle or suffering, they are desperate for help and relief, and the prospect of a long, slow journey is beyond daunting. But at the same time, you have to be honest. There is no quick fix.

I asked Justin to give me a brief overview of his own journey. He told me he started with the Wounded Warrior Project, then moved on to therapy, attended some weekend retreats for veterans, and spent a week in a group therapy program.

Throughout his journey, he has discovered therapies, modalities, tools, and processes that work for him, and he has focused on integrating these into his daily life. This is how your healing path becomes a well-being path: the integration of, and adherence to, a new way of living.

CONTINUING THE JOURNEY

As a follow-up, I asked Justin to share how he keeps himself from wandering off the path, or worse, turning around and going backward.

First of all, he says he got into the work he does now for "selfish" reasons, to create a form of accountability for himself. He knew being immersed in this world of healing and well-being would be a powerful incentive to keep doing his own work. He says warriors have a powerful bullshit detector, so if you're going to do this work, you have to continually work on yourself, which he does.

He also continues with therapy when he recognizes he needs it. Additionally, he sought out his own healing network, outside of The Battle Within, because he knew he couldn't lean on the organization he runs for his healing.

At work, he *is* the helper, so he knew he needed to find places where he could turn for help. He got connected with professional networks that filled some of that void, and that helped immensely. He shared with me that last year was a very rough year for him, both personally and professionally, and says those networks helped him through all of it.

What he knows now was that he allowed himself to get depleted last year, but he didn't realize it was happening until he was in pretty bad shape. Once he became aware, he reevaluated and got focused on finding balance. This involved leaning into his support networks, integrating mindful moments into his days, journaling, taking walks, and using other tools that bring him peace and stability.

ADVICE AND TIPS

When I asked Justin if he has advice for people who haven't stepped onto a healing path yet, or those who are struggling to stay the course, the first thing he said was, "Personal goals are crucial. There has to be a balance between work and personal life."

To help himself achieve this balance, Justin established a personal mission statement, and from that, he derived personal goals and intentions. He has a list of six personal intentions that he has determined to focus on for the year, but each day he chooses only one or two of those, which keeps this process from overwhelming him.

Every morning, he reads his personal mission statement and writes down a couple of goals or intentions for the day. Then, at night, he reviews his day and quickly journals about his experiences from the day. As he explained this to me, he emphasized that it's a very brief exercise. He structured it that way on purpose so it would stick.

He cautions people that starting a new process like this will probably be uncomfortable in the beginning. "But stick with it," he encourages. "Set a goal and build from there. Try committing to the new habit for ten days. Then evaluate and set your next goal, for maybe thirty days, and keep going."

Something important to note is that a healing journey will involve lifestyle changes, which can be challenging, because we humans are creatures of habit. But I promise, the benefits will be worth the effort.

THE FUTURE OF WARRIOR WELLNESS

Justin believes it's important for agencies and organizations that do this warrior wellness work to support each other and work together to help prevent relapse and recidivism. He works toward the goal of creating a connected network that benefits all warriors by creating a true continuum of care and a broader structure to help support their journey.

He envisions an organized community of organizations working together to ensure the success of this well warrior movement, like a Mayo Clinic for warrior mental health.

If we expand on Justin's vision, we can imagine a world equipped with these centers or communities that all form relationships with each other and cooperatively and continuously funnel people to the right next program or service for them. My motto is, if we can imagine it, it's possible.

TRENDS

Something Justin has witnessed over the past several years is people completing a program like The Battle Within, and then going on to advocate and help others feel safe and more comfortable reaching out for help. He's so proud of the alumni he's seen step into that role. It means they've taken their healing seriously, improved their own lives, and then offered themselves as an example to peers.

He's also proud of the many graduates of the program who are doing better and keep doing their own inner work. They will often say to The Battle Within staff, "You guys saved my life." And while it's gratifying to help people, Justin says all the credit goes to the individual for being strong enough to survive and soft enough to do the healing work.

One potentially negative trend we touched on was the danger of helping other people instead of doing your own work. Just like anything else, helping others can become an addiction, and an avoidance tactic. We can get so caught up and "busy" supporting others that we neglect ourselves. It might be a cliché, but you can't pour from an empty pitcher. Also, remember, as Justin said, the warrior bullshit detector is pretty accurate. If you're depleted and unwell, a warrior will know.

Justin is a great example of a warrior who chose a healing path, continues to walk the way of well-being, and is dedicated to helping others on their journey to wellness.

Now, on to the peersources!

PEERSOURCES

Here is a full list of the modalities, tools, and support mechanisms mentioned by the warriors I interviewed for this book. I hope this list helps you choose and test out some new skills, therapies, and lifestyle choices.

- Meditation

- Mindfulness

- Breathing

- Contemplative practices

- Counseling/therapy—private and group therapy

- EMDR therapy

- Journaling/writing

- Talking

- Listening

- Exercise/fitness/staying active

- Having the right people around you

- Books/reading—for pleasure, and self-help books

- Health and wellness apps

- Being in nature

- Connecting with other trauma survivors

- Understanding how trauma affects your brain and body

- Truly understanding empathy and knowing when one is not operating from a place of empathy

- Support system

- Peer support

- Yoga

- Pet therapy

- Stellate ganglion block

- Studying and understanding neuroscience

- Studying and understanding trauma

- Telling your story

- Staying away from alcohol
- Healthy diet
- Limit intake of news
- Limit social media
- Creativity/a creative outlet

- Neurofeedback
- Hobbies
- Animals, pets
- Solitude, peace and quiet
- Treatment programs

I'm going to wrap up this book by providing crisis numbers and a directory full of books, articles, podcasts, apps, and other resources I think you'll find useful. Remember, healing is not a one-and-done proposition. To achieve and maintain well-being, you'll have to integrate wellness practices into your life with consistency.

I hope I, and the gracious warriors in this book, have helped inspire you and that our stories will motivate you to take care of yourself, seek help, and accept support.

CHAPTER 22

CRISIS RESOURCES

*(If you or someone you know is in
immediate danger, call 911 now)*

———

FOR ALL WARRIORS

988 SUICIDE AND CRISIS HOTLINE

Nationwide, free, confidential support for people in distress.

Dial 988

SUICIDE.ORG

Suicide prevention, awareness, and support.

www.suicide.org
1-800-SUICIDE (1-800-784-2433)

CRISIS TEXT LINE

Connect with a volunteer crisis counselor by text, talk, or WhatsApp.

www.crisistextline.org
Text HOME to 741741

SAFE CALL NOW

Twenty-four-hour confidential crisis referral service staffed by first responders.

For public safety professionals, emergency services personnel, and family members.

Assistance with treatment options for mental health, substance abuse, and other personal issues.

www.safecallnowusa.org
1-206-459-3020

FOR LAW ENFORCEMENT

COPLINE

Law enforcement officer hotline for officers and their family members.

Guarantees confidentiality and anonymity.

Lines answered by trained, competent, retired officers.

www.copline.org
1-800-267-5463

FOR FIRE/EMS

FIRE/EMS HELPLINE

Free, confidential.
www.nvfc.org/helpline
1-888-731-3473

SHARE THE LOAD PROGRAM

A behavioral health directory of resources.

*www.nvfc.org/*help

FOR VETERANS

VETERANS CRISIS LINE

A 24/7 confidential crisis line.
Call, text, or chat online.

www.veteranscrisisline.net
Dial 988, then press 1
Text 83825

CHAPTER 23

RESOURCE DIRECTORY

Books, articles, podcasts, apps, and more to help you begin your journey to well-being

---

I'd like to extend a warm thank you to MJ Fievre, of Mango Publishing Group, for her help in compiling and organizing this resource directory. I'm grateful for your assistance, MJ!

In this section you'll find:

- Books: An essential reading list to deepen your knowledge of stress management, mindfulness, healing, and wellness.

- Articles: Selected writings offering additional insights and up-to-date research relevant to your wellness journey.

- Podcasts: Thought-provoking and informative podcasts focused on wellness, offering an opportunity to learn from experts as well as peers in your field.

- Apps: Hand-picked applications that are designed to support mental health, facilitate mindfulness, and relieve stress.

- Websites/Blogs: A collection of useful websites and blogs offering resources, personal experiences, advice, and the latest information on wellness, mindfulness and more.

- Inspiring Talks: Quick boosts of understanding and knowledge from researchers, scientists, and others.

- Programs, Courses, and Workshops: Options for in-person or virtual classes or programs for warriors seeking support.

- Support Networks: An array of support groups, community organizations, and online communities where warriors can connect, discuss, and provide mutual support.

- Equipment/Tools: Recommendations for equipment and tools that aid in practicing mindfulness, managing stress, and enhancing overall wellness.

This guide is designed to provide insight, information, options, and ideas to help you make your way toward improved mental health, enhanced resilience, and a more balanced way of living. I hope you'll explore the list and find ways to integrate healthy practices, habits, and tools into your life.

BOOKS

The Body Keeps the Score—Bessel van der Kolk: A book about how trauma affects the body and mind. It explains how trauma can cause physical and emotional problems and provides healing methods.

The Mindfulness for Warriors Handbook—A book that combines a candid and personal memoir with insightful warrior interviews and a simple guide to meditation and mindfulness.

Struggle Well: Thriving in the Aftermath of Trauma—Ken Falke, Josh Goldberg: This book is tailored to veterans and focuses on teaching combat veterans specifically how to achieve post-traumatic growth.

Bulletproof Spirit—Captain Dan Willis: A book about developing resilience in adversity. It provides practical tips on how to overcome challenges and become more resilient.

Emotional Intelligence—Daniel Goleman: A book about how emotional intelligence can help you succeed. It explains what emotional intelligence is, why it's essential, and how to develop it.

Emotional Survival for Law Enforcement—Kevin Gilmartin, PhD: A book about how law enforcement officers can cope with the stress of their job. It provides practical tips on how to manage stress and maintain mental health.

First Responder Resilience—Tania Glenn: A book about how first responders can develop resilience in adversity. It provides practical tips on how to overcome challenges and become more resilient.

Haunted by Combat—Stanley Krippner PhD and Daryl S. Paulson: A book that offers insights into the realities of PTSD and combat trauma, and how symptoms may pervade even the most mundane of daily activities. In a new epilogue, the authors offer data about treatments and resources that both PTSD sufferers and their families and friends will value.

I Love a Firefighter—Ellen Kirschman: A book about how to cope with the unique challenges of being in a relationship with a firefighter. It provides practical tips on how to maintain a healthy relationship.

Increasing Resilience in Police and Emergency Personnel—Stephanie M. Conn: A book about how police officers and emergency personnel can develop resilience in the face of adversity. It provides practical tips on how to overcome challenges and become more resilient.

Invisible Storm—Jason Kander: Former army intelligence officer Jason Kander has written the book he himself needed in the most painful moments of his PTSD.

Man's Search for Meaning—Viktor E. Frankl: Although not specifically targeted at first responders, Frankl's classic work can provide profound insights on resilience and finding purpose in the midst of suffering, themes that may resonate with those in high-stress, trauma-exposed professions.

Mindsight—Dr. Daniel Siegel: A book about how the mind works and how we can change it. It explains what mindsight is, why it's essential, and how to develop it.

The Power of Vulnerability—Brené Brown: A book about how vulnerability can help us connect with others and live more fulfilling lives. It explains vulnerability, its importance, and how to embrace it.

The Daily Stoic: 366 Meditations on Wisdom, Perseverance, and the Art of Living—Ryan Holiday: This book features insights from Marcus Aurelius, Seneca, and other great stoic philosophers.

Relentless Courage—Michael Sugrue and Shauna Springer, PhD: A book about how veterans can overcome PTSD and other mental health issues. It provides practical tips on how to manage symptoms and improve mental health.

A Daily Dose of Now—Nita Sweeney: A book that delivers tiny doses of mindfulness in an insightful, practical, and relatable way. Perfect for skeptics, newbies, or pros.

Resilient—Dr. Rick Hanson: A book about how to develop resilience in the face of adversity. It provides practical tips on how to overcome challenges and become more resilient.

Trauma Stewardship—by Laura van Dernoot Lipsky: This book offers practical tools for those who work to alleviate the suffering of others and could be very applicable for first responders.

The Power of Now—Eckhart Tolle: This book has been around a long time and has helped millions of people understand the power and importance of the present moment, and how this relates to meditation and mindfulness.

The Upside of Stress—Kelly McGonigal: A book about how stress can benefit us. It explains what stress is, why it's essential, and how we can use it to our advantage.

10% Happier—Dan Harris: A true story of a news anchor who found meditation after having a panic attack on live TV. He shares his journey and how meditation helped him reduce stress and improve his life.

ARTICLES

The following curated list of articles can significantly contribute to your knowledge about essential topics like mindfulness, stress management, the benefits of yoga and meditation, overcoming mental health stigma, and trauma-informed leadership. Each article provides a unique perspective on the challenges warriors face, their mental health needs, and the practices they can adopt to lead healthier lives. This diverse collection aims to provide you with a comprehensive understanding of the subject, incorporating viewpoints from different authors, domains, and experiences.

Goerling, Richard. "The Case for Mindfulness in Policing." Calibrepress.com. May 23, 2018. www.calibrepress.com/2018/05/the-case-for-mindfulness-in-policing

Baum, Naomi L. "Demystifying Mindfulness." *Fire Rescue Magazine.* June 26, 2017. https://www.firefighternation.com/firerescue/demystifying-mindfulness/

McGreevey, Sue. "Eight Weeks to a Better Brain." *The Harvard Gazette.* January 21, 2011. news.harvard.edu/gazette/story/2011/01/eight-weeks-to-a-better-brain

Luster, Rodney. "First Responders and Mental Health: When Heroes Need Rescuing." *Psychiatric Times.* September 9, 2022. www.psychiatrictimes.com/view/first-responders-and-mental-health-when-heroes-need-rescuing

Hummell, Wendy. "How yoga and meditation helped sharpen my aim." *Police1.* August 20, 2018. www.police1.com/police-training/articles/how-yoga-and-meditation-helped-sharpen-my-aim-U1igYyNBTQ1RSINh

Pittaro, Michael. "Mental Health Care for First Responders: Confronting the stigma and barriers to treatment." *Psychology Today.* July 3, 2019. www.psychologytoday.com/us/blog/the-crime-and-justice-doctor/201907/mental-health-care-first-responders

Wolkin, Jennifer. "The Science of Trauma, Mindfulness, and PTSD." Mindful.org. June 15, 2016. www.mindful.org/the-science-of-trauma-mindfulness-ptsd

Bustos, Cathy. "Trauma-Informed Leadership." *Police Chief* magazine. May 24, 2023. www.policechiefmagazine.org/trauma-informed-leadership

PODCASTS

Welcome to the podcast section of our resource guide. Podcasts are an excellent medium for learning, growth, and support, as they offer a unique blend of storytelling, expert insights, and actionable advice.

Our list encompasses podcasts that offer a broad perspective on the life and experiences of first responders. They delve into various topics, including mental health, physical fitness, resilience, leadership, stress management, and career development. Although not all these podcasts are tailored specifically for first responders, they present themes and discussions that can benefit their well-being and professional development.

- *Guns & Yoga*: Host Wendy Hummell, a twenty-five-year law enforcement professional and yogini, examines all aspects of first responder wellness. Named a 2022 Top 12 podcast by *Police1*.

- *The Squad Room*: This podcast is designed for law enforcement professionals. It explores mental health, physical fitness, leadership, and career development topics.

- *The Washdown*: Firefighters and other first responders discuss mental health, wellness, and other topics of interest.

- *Veteran Chat Project*: A podcast that supports veteran mental health.

- *The Alpha Human Podcast*: While not explicitly focused on first responders, this podcast shares stories of resilience, strength, and overcoming adversity—themes that can resonate with and inspire first responders.

- *Crisis Intervention Team (CIT) Minute*: Focused on reducing the stigma around mental health discussions, this podcast addresses specific issues first responders face, like PTSD, and presents various ways to manage these challenges.

- *Dear Chiefs Podcast*: This podcast is designed for fire service leaders. It offers insights into leadership, management, and organizational culture.

- *The First Responder Fitness Podcast*: A podcast dedicated to physical fitness and wellness strategies for first responders, offering ways to maintain optimal physical health while handling the high-stress environment of first responder work.

- *First Responder Trauma Counselors*: This podcast explores mental health topics and trauma, especially those experienced by first responders, offering advice from professionals and sharing stories from other first responders.

- *Health, Nutrition, and Functional Medicine*: This podcast is designed to help first responders improve their health through nutrition and functional medicine. It offers insights into how nutrition can help manage stress and improve well-being.

- *Inside EMS*: A podcast for and about EMS professionals, discussing issues like mental health, job-related stress, and methods to cope with them. It also offers insights into the latest EMS news and trends.

- *Meditative Story*: Although not specifically for first responders, this podcast combines inspirational stories narrators tell with meditative music to induce a mindful state, potentially useful for relaxation and stress reduction.

- *No One Fights Alone*: This podcast is designed for first responders. It explores mental health, physical fitness, leadership, and career development topics.

- *Behind the Shield*: A mental health and support resource for emergency service professionals and their families from James Geering.

- *The Warrior Wellness Podcast*: This podcast is for military members, veterans, and first responders, focusing on fitness, health, nutrition, and biohacking. Its mission is to introduce America's heroes to lifestyle habits and hacks to help them live healthier, happier lives.

APPS

The apps listed below cater to various aspects of mental health and well-being. Each of these apps offers valuable tools and strategies that can help you navigate your unique challenges. However, these apps are not a substitute for professional help when it is needed. They are part of a broader wellness strategy that includes professional mental health support, social connection, physical activity, adequate rest, and other healthy lifestyle choices.

- Insight Timer: This app features over 80,000 free guided meditations, music tracks, and talks from mindfulness experts. You can choose sessions according to your available time, varying from one minute to several hours. It also offers an advanced timer for silent meditations and bedtime stories to help you sleep.

- 10% Happier: Based on the bestselling book by Dan Harris, this app offers a wide range of guided meditations, including courses specifically designed for coping with stress and anxiety.

- Aura: Provides mindfulness meditations, life coaching, stories, and music, all personalized based on the mood you select when you open the app.

- Breathe2Relax: This app provides detailed information on the effects of stress on the body and instructions on stress management exercises, such as diaphragmatic breathing.

- Calm: Calm is a leading app for meditation and sleep, offering guided meditations, Sleep Stories, breathing programs, stretching exercises, and relaxing music. The app is designed to help users reduce stress and anxiety, improve focus, and get better sleep.

- Headspace: Headspace offers guided meditations, animations, articles, and videos, all in the distinct Headspace style. The app covers topics like stress, sleep focus, and anxiety, offering courses on mindful living and even workout routines.

- Meditopia: Meditopia is a meditation app that helps users reduce stress, sleep well, build mental resilience, and experience long-term relaxation. The app offers over a thousand guided meditations on stress, anxiety, happiness, self-love, focus, calm, and personal growth.

- MyLife Meditation (formerly Stop, Breathe & Think): A meditation app that allows you to check in with your emotions and then recommends short, guided meditations, yoga, and acupressure videos, tuned to how you feel.

- PTSD Coach: Created by the Veterans Administration, PTSD Coach offers self-help strategies and resources to manage trauma-related symptoms.

- Sanvello: An app designed to help manage stress, anxiety, and depression through cognitive-behavioral therapy, mindfulness meditation, and other mental health practices.

- Sleep Cycle: Focused on improving sleep quality, the app analyzes sleep patterns and wakes users during their lightest sleep phase to ensure they wake feeling rested.

- Smiling Mind: A mindfulness app developed by psychologists and educators that offers a range of programs for all ages, including programs to assist with sleep, relationships, and performance.

- Streaks: Streaks is a to-do list that helps you form good habits. You can customize the app to help you maintain a streak in any activity, such as meditation, exercise, or reading. It's an excellent tool for motivating consistent behaviors that contribute to wellness.

- The Resilience Project: This app provides practical, evidence-based mental health strategies to build resilience and happiness. It offers activities to help you remain calm and mindful, develop gratitude and empathy, and increase emotional literacy.

- Tide—Sleep & Meditation: This app combines natural sounds with mindfulness practices to improve sleep, focus, relaxation, and meditation. It offers features like a focus timer, breathing guide, and meditation sessions.

WEBSITES/BLOGS

In today's digital age, a wealth of knowledge and support is just a click away. Numerous websites and blogs provide valuable information, support, and resources for warriors and their families dealing with stress, trauma, and the unique challenges they face. These online platforms offer a range of insights—from expert advice and evidence-based strategies to personal stories of overcoming adversity.

Please note that the content and views expressed on these websites are their own. Always consult with a healthcare professional for personal medical advice.

- Pause First Academy (www.pausefirst.com): This organization is owned and operated by Kim Colegrove. Visit the website to learn more about their in-person and online training. Visit the online academy to view on-demand courses and content created specifically for first responders. (Options available for individuals and organizations) (academy.pausefirst.com)

- Firefighter Behavioral Health Alliance (FBHA) (www.ffbha. org): This organization is dedicated to providing behavioral health workshops to fire departments and EMS organizations across the globe.

- First Responder Wellness (www.firstresponder-wellness. com/blog): This blog provides wellness resources specifically tailored to first responders, including mental health support and advice.

- Wounded Warrior Project (www.woundedwarriorproject. org): This organization provides an array of programs to help warriors recover.

- That Peer Support Couple (www.cathyandjavi.com): Cathy and Javier Bustos, both former law enforcement, are International Critical Incident Stress Foundation (ICISF) instructors that offer counseling and peer support for individuals, couples, and organizations.

- Save a Warrior (www.saveawarrior.org): This organization is dedicated to preventing veteran suicide and helping veterans through their groundbreaking, comprehensive program.

- Headspace Blog (www.headspace.com/blog): The blog of the popular meditation app focusing on mindfulness, meditation, and related topics.

- Mindful (www.mindful.org): This website is an excellent resource on mindfulness practices, research, and advice.

- The Mindful Badge Initiative (www.mindfulbadge.com): This organization provides mindfulness training specifically for law enforcement and first responders.

- National Alliance on Mental Illness (NAMI) Blog (www.nami.org/blogs): The NAMI blog provides a range of mental health resources, including posts focused on first responders.

- PoliceOne (www.policeone.com/health-fitness): This website is a comprehensive resource for law enforcement professionals, whose health and fitness section covers physical and mental well-being.

- Psychology Today (www.psychologytoday.com): Contains a vast range of articles from professionals about mental health, self-improvement, and behavioral science, including trauma and stress management.

- The Resilience Project (www.resilienceproject.com.au): A resource providing practical, evidence-based mental health strategies to build resilience.

- Tema Conter Memorial Trust (www.tema.ca): This Canadian organization provides resources for first responders dealing with mental stress and trauma.

INSPIRATIONAL TALKS & MINDFUL DISCUSSIONS

"The Power of Vulnerability" by Brené Brown on TEDTalks: While not specific to first responders, this talk on vulnerability can benefit those dealing with emotional stress and trauma.

"All It Takes Is 10 Mindful Minutes" by Andy Puddicombe on TEDTalks: A brief, engaging talk about the value of taking a few minutes daily for mindful meditation.

"How to Make Stress Your Friend" by Kelly McGonigal on TEDTalks: Psychologist Kelly McGonigal urges us to see stress as a positive and introduces us to an unsung mechanism for stress reduction: reaching out to others.

"Building Resilience" by Lucy Hone on TEDxChristchurch: This presentation discusses strategies for building resilience in the face of adversity.

"Depression, the Secret We Share" by Andrew Solomon on TEDTalks: A profound talk on understanding and coping with depression.

"Grit: The Power of Passion and Perseverance" by Angela Lee Duckworth on TEDTalks: An insightful talk about the power of resilience and perseverance.

"How Mindfulness Changes the Emotional Life of Our Brains" by Richard J. Davidson, on TEDxSanFrancisco: Renowned neuroscientist Richard J. Davidson discusses the impact of mindfulness on the brain's emotional response.

"Happiness TED Talk" by Sean Achor, on TEDxBloomington: *New York Times* bestselling author Sean Achor is one of the world's leading experts on the connection between happiness and success.

"Mindfulness and Neural Integration" by Daniel Siegel, MD, at TEDxStudioCityED: A discussion on how mindfulness impacts the brain and can lead to neural integration, improving mental health and well-being.

"Why We All Need to Practice Emotional First Aid" by Guy Winch on TEDTalks: A TED talk focusing on the importance of taking care of our emotional health as we do our physical health.

"Yoga for First Responders" by Olivia Kvitne Mead, YouTube: This is a quick introduction to the benefits of yoga for first responders by the program's founder.

PROGRAMS, COURSES, AND WORKSHOPS

- Pause First Academy (www.pausefirst.com): This organization is owned and operated by Kim Colegrove. Visit the website to learn more about their in-person and online training. Visit the online academy to view on-demand courses and content created specifically for first responders. (Options available for individuals and organizations) (www.academy.pausefirst.com)

- The Battle Within (thebattlewithin.org): The program offers a five-day group therapy program created by fellow warriors to help others suffering from PTS(D) understand the traumas they have endured in service to others, provide an introduction to integrative tools that set the stage for healing, and develop a community of support. It also offers ninety-day classes built to fit into warriors' busy lives and provided by partner organizations that develop into habits the tools introduced during the Revenant Journey, such as fitness, equine, meditation, spiritual, nutrition, and arts programs. This program is donor funded. There is no cost for a warrior to attend.

- West Coast Post-Trauma Retreat (www.frsn.org/west-coast-post-trauma-retreat.html): A residential program designed to help current and retired first responders regain control over their lives.

- Firefighter Behavioral Health Alliance Workshops (https://www.ffbha.org/workshops/workshops-offered/): These workshops provide behavioral health workshops to firefighters, their families, and departments.

- Save A Warrior (saveawarrior.org): The program offers a holistic approach to healing combat veterans and first responders who have PTSD. It includes peer-to-peer support groups, outdoor activities such as hiking and camping trips, and mindfulness meditation.

- First Responders First (firstrespondersfirst.com): Veterans and first responders have designed the program for veterans and first responders struggling with primary mental health, trauma, PTSD, addiction, depression, and co-occurring disorders.

- Help for Our Heroes (helpforourheroes.com): The program is designed to help veterans and first responders struggling with primary mental health, trauma, PTSD, addiction, depression, and co-occurring disorders.

- Mental Health First Aid for Fire and EMS by the National Council for Behavioral Health (https://afsp.org/mental-health-first-aid/): This course helps fire and EMS personnel understand mental health and offers strategies to help those experiencing a mental health crisis.

- Mindful Badge Initiative (https://www.mindfulbadge.com/): Offers mindfulness training for law enforcement and first responders.

- Mindfulness-Based Stress Reduction (MBSR) online course by Palouse Mindfulness (https://palousemindfulness.com/): A free, internationally recognized program designed to assist people in dealing with physical and emotional stress.

- The Resilient First Responder by Dr. Stephanie Conn (https://firstresponderpsychology.com/): Provides first responders with the knowledge, techniques, and skills to build resilience and prevent trauma.

- Responder Resilience Training by Acadia Healthcare (https://www.acadiahealthcare.com/programming-treatment/first-responders/resiliency-training/): These are comprehensive programs designed to promote resiliency among first responders and healthcare professionals.

- Stress Management and Resiliency Training (SMART) for First Responders (https://www.heart911.org/programs/smart-program): This is a course offered in conjunction with the Benson-Henry Institute for Mind Body Medicine that provides evidence-based strategies for stress management.

- Veteran's PATH (veteranspath.org): The program offers mindfulness-based retreats for veterans and their families. It also offers online courses on mindfulness meditation and other topics related to mental health.

- "Demystifying Meditation and Mindfulness for Criminal Justice Professionals" with instructor Kim Colegrove: Available on the Justice Clearinghouse website, www.justiceclearinghouse.com/resource/demystifying-meditation-and-mindfulness-for-criminal-justice-professionals/.

- "Tools to Manage the Stress Response" with instructor Wendy Hummell: On the Justice Clearinghouse website, www.justiceclearinghouse.com/resource/tools-to-manage-the-stress-response/.

- Yoga for First Responders (https://www.yogaforfirstresponders.org/): YFFR offers yoga and mindfulness training designed to help first responders process stress, build resilience, and enhance job performance.

- First Responder Mental Health and Wellness Conference (https://www.1strc.org/): This conference focuses on the challenges first responders face, discussing the importance of mental health and well-being in these high-stress professions.

- Global Resilience Summit (https://www.globalresiliencesummit.org/): This summit focuses on building resilience, a crucial trait for first responders. It often includes talks on mindfulness as a tool for resilience.

- 1st Responder Conferences (www.1strc.org): Nationwide conferences for first responders focused on the emotional, physical, and spiritual well-being of the public safety workforce.

- International Conference on Mindfulness (https://home.mindfulness-network.org/): This annual event offers a platform for exchanging knowledge related to mindfulness techniques, practice, and research, often attracting professionals, educators, and practitioners from across the globe.

- International Symposium for Contemplative Research (https://www.iscrconference.org/): An interdisciplinary conference that brings together academics, educators, and practitioners to discuss the latest research in mindfulness and meditation.

- Meditative Mindfulness Congress: An international event focusing on meditation practices and their implementation in various fields, including high-stress professions.

- Mindful Leader Summit (https://www.mindfulleader.org/mindfulness-events): An event focusing on integrating mindfulness into leadership, beneficial for leaders in first responder organizations.

- Mindful Society Conference (https://www.mindfulinstitute. org/): This event explores the application of mindfulness in a wide range of societal sectors, including healthcare, education, and public safety.

- Mindfulness Expo (https://mindfulnessexpo.com/about/): A significant event hosting various workshops, speakers, and vendors centered around mindfulness practices.

- National Alliance on Mental Illness (NAMI) conferences (https://convention.nami.org/): While these events cover a broad range of mental health topics, there are often sessions dedicated to the mental health and wellness of first responders, including mindfulness strategies.

- Wisdom 2.0 Conference (https://www.wisdom2summit. com/): This conference brings together people from various disciplines to explore how we can live with mindfulness, wisdom, and compassion in the digital age.

SUPPORT NETWORKS

A support network can serve as a lifeline for warriors, offering a safe space to share experiences, seek advice, and find comfort in knowing you are not alone. These platforms can be particularly beneficial for those dealing with stress, trauma, and other mental health issues common in high-pressure professions. Whether you're looking for an online forum, a face-to-face support group, or a community organization, you will find a resource here that can provide the support you need.

- First H.E.L.P. (www.1sthelp.org): This organization is working to reduce mental health stigma for first responders through education and awareness.

- American Foundation for Suicide Prevention (AFSP) Peer Support: Connects individuals who have experienced a suicide loss.

- EMDR International Association—Trauma Recovery Networks: While not a traditional support group, these networks offer resources and connections for individuals interested in EMDR therapy, a treatment often used for PTSD.

- Mindful Badge Initiative: Offers mindfulness training and resources for law enforcement, including online support groups and sessions.

- NAMI's Homefront: An online and in-person educational program for families, caregivers, and friends of military service members and veterans dealing with mental health conditions.

- National Police Suicide Foundation Support Groups: This foundation offers various resources for police officers and their families, including support groups.

- Online Grief Support Forums: Online communities where people dealing with grief can share their experiences and support each other.

- Survivors of Suicide Loss Support Groups: These groups provide a comforting environment for individuals who have lost a loved one to suicide.

COMMUNITY ORGANIZATIONS

- The Code Green Campaign: A first responder-oriented mental health advocacy and education organization.

- EMDR International Association (EMDRIA): Promotes health and growth for individuals who have experienced trauma, including first responders, through Eye Movement Desensitization and Reprocessing (EMDR) therapy.

- Firefighter Behavioral Health Alliance (FBHA): Dedicated to educating emergency services personnel and their families about behavioral health issues including, but not limited to, depression, PTSD, and suicide ideation.

- First Responder Support Network (FRSN): Offers educational treatment programs for first responders and their families.

- National Alliance on Mental Illness (NAMI): Provides resources and support for those struggling with mental health issues, including a particular focus on first responders.

- National Emergency Services Wellness Institute (NESWI): Aims to improve the mental, physical, and spiritual well-being of emergency service professionals.

- Tema Conter Memorial Trust: Provides training and resources for public safety and military personnel dealing with occupational stress and PTSD.

EQUIPMENT/TOOLS

Below, you'll find stress management and mindfulness equipment and tools to enhance and support your journey to well-being.

- Anti-Stress Comfort Wrap: Heat this wrap in the microwave and then wrap it around your neck and shoulders for deep tissue relaxation.

- Essential Oils/Diffuser: Essential oils like lavender and chamomile can be calming and used with meditation and relaxation practices.

- Journal: A mindfulness journal can help track progress and experiences during meditation and mindfulness exercises.

- Meditation Cushion or Bench: To ensure comfortable sitting during meditation practices.

- Mindfulness Cards: These cards provide prompts and exercises to help incorporate mindfulness into the daily routine.

- Muse Headband: A tool used for biofeedback during meditation. The headband gives real-time feedback on brain activity, heart rate, breathing, and body movements to assist in developing a consistent and effective meditation practice.

- Noise-Canceling Headphones: These can be useful for blocking out distractions during meditation or relaxation practices.

- Weighted Blanket: Some people find that using a weighted blanket can have a calming effect, reducing anxiety and promoting better sleep.

- Yoga Mat: Useful for practicing yoga and body scan meditation.

FINAL THOUGHTS

I hope this book, the stories, and these resource lists will inspire you to step onto a healing path or will help bolster and support your current well-being journey. At the very least, if you've felt alone, may this book cause you to realize you are not.

You aren't broken, damaged, or weak. You are human. Please embrace self-care, allow yourself grace, and find ways to tend to your invisible wounds.

My very best to you, warrior. Thank you for your service to humanity.

To learn more about Kim Colegrove's work or Pause First Academy, you can reach Kim at:

kimcolegrove@pausefirst.com

ABOUT THE AUTHOR

Kim Colegrove is the author of *Mindfulness for Warriors* and *The Mindfulness for Warriors Handbook* and the owner of Pause First Academy, an organization that provides wellness and resilience training for society's warriors, protectors, guardians, and healers. She's an international presenter on the topics of meditation, mindfulness, and warrior wellness, and, in 2022, she was awarded the Mid-America CIT (Critical Incident Team) Teacher of the Year award.

Colegrove is a veteran meditator with over forty-five years of experience. She previously worked as a corporate meditation instructor and consultant. Her corporate clients include Garmin International, United Way, Department of Veterans Affairs, The National Court Reporters Association, and many others.

In 2014, Kim lost her husband, former police officer and Federal Agent David Colegrove, to suicide, less than three months after he retired from a thirty-year law enforcement career. After her husband's death, Colegrove began educating herself about the mental and emotional impacts of law enforcement work. When she learned how prevalent chronic stress, anxiety, depression, silent suffering, and suicide are across all first responder professions, she decided she wanted to do something to help.

She started offering workshops and writing on the topic of first responder mental health and wellness, and her work quickly expanded to include not only first responders, but veterans, corrections employees, mental health personnel, and other professionals who are regularly exposed to trauma.

She now works with a team of culturally competent instructors who offer education nationwide and internationally by speaking at conferences, offering continuing education, and providing in-service training. The team also offers web-based learning. Individuals and organizations across the country are benefitting from Pause First Academy's Premier Membership, an online subscription service that delivers on-demand courses and content focused on wellness, resilience, and work-life balance.

Kim's mission is to help normalize mental health support and wellness education for all warriors by delivering information, education, and training.

Mango Publishing, established in 2014, publishes an eclectic list of books by diverse authors—both new and established voices—on topics ranging from business, personal growth, women's empowerment, LGBTQ+ studies, health, and spirituality to history, popular culture, time management, decluttering, lifestyle, mental wellness, aging, and sustainable living. We were named 2019 *and* 2020's #1 fastest growing independent publisher by *Publishers Weekly*. Our success is driven by our main goal, which is to publish high-quality books that will entertain readers as well as make a positive difference in their lives.

Our readers are our most important resource; we value your input, suggestions, and ideas. We'd love to hear from you—after all, we are publishing books for you!

Please stay in touch with us and follow us at:

Facebook: Mango Publishing

Twitter: @MangoPublishing

Instagram: @MangoPublishing

LinkedIn: Mango Publishing

Pinterest: Mango Publishing

Newsletter: mangopublishinggroup.com/newsletter

Join us on Mango's journey to reinvent publishing, one book at a time.

Printed in the USA
CPSIA information can be obtained
at www.ICGtesting.com
JSHW03083821l223
54085JS00008B/8